The Philosophy of the *Yogasūtra*

Bloomsbury Introductions to World Philosophies

Series Editor:
Monika Kirloskar-Steinbach

Assistant Series Editor:
Leah Kalmanson

Regional Editors:
Nader El-Bizri, James Madaio, Sarah A. Mattice, Takeshi Morisato, Pascah Mungwini, Mickaella Perina, Omar Rivera and Georgina Stewart

Bloomsbury Introductions to World Philosophies delivers primers reflecting exciting new developments in the trajectory of world philosophies. Instead of privileging a single philosophical approach as the basis of comparison, the series provides a platform for diverse philosophical perspectives to accommodate the different dimensions of cross-cultural philosophizing. While introducing thinkers, texts and themes emanating from different world philosophies, each book, in an imaginative and path-breaking way, makes clear how it departs from a conventional treatment of the subject matter.

Titles in the Series:

A Practical Guide to World Philosophies, by Monika Kirloskar-Steinbach and Leah Kalmanson
Daya Krishna and Twentieth-Century Indian Philosophy, by Daniel Raveh
Māori Philosophy, by Georgina Tuari Stewart
Philosophy of Science and the Kyoto School, by Dean Anthony Brink
Tanabe Hajime and the Kyoto School, by Takeshi Morisato
African Philosophy, by Pascah Mungwini
The Philosophy of the Brahma-sūtra, by Aleksandar Uskokov
Sikh Philosophy, by Arvind-Pal Singh Mandair
The Life and Thought of Henry Odera Oruka, by Gail M. Presbey

The Philosophy of the *Yogasūtra*

An Introduction

Karen O'Brien-Kop

BLOOMSBURY
NEW DELHI • LONDON • OXFORD • NEW YORK • SYDNEY

Bloomsbury Publishing India
DDA Complex, LSC Building No. 4 Second Floor, Pocket C – 6 & 7,
Vasant Kunj , New Delhi 110070

BLOOMSBURY, Bloomsbury Academic India and the Diana
logo are trademarks of Bloomsbury Publishing Plc

First published in India 2024
First published in Great Britain 2023

Series design by Louise Dugdale
Cover image © Govindanmarudhai / Getty Images

This edition is published with permission from Bloomsbury Publishing Plc.
50 Bedford Square, London WC1B3DP

A catalogue record for this book is available from the British Library.
A catalog record for this book is available from the Library of Congress.
ISBN: 978-93-61315-56-5
For sale in the Indian subcontinent only

Exclusively distributed in the Indian subcontinent by
Manohar Publishers & Distributors
4753/23, Ansari Road
Darya Ganj, New Delhi 110002
Tel.: 23284848, 23289100
Email: sales@manoharbooks.com, manoharbooks@gmail.com

Series: Bloomsbury Introductions to World Philosophies
Typeset by Integra Software Services Pvt. Ltd.
Printed and bound in India by Replika Press Pvt. Ltd

Contents

List of figures and tables

Figures

Tables

Acknowledgements

Thank you to Professor Monika Kirloskar-Steinbach for commissioning this series and to Dr James Madaio for initiating this title. Thank you to Professor Geoffrey Ashton for providing illuminating feedback on a draft and to all of the reviewers who commented on various stages of the proposal or draft. I was grateful to be part of the teaching and learning environment in the Religions and Philosophies Department at SOAS University of London for the early stages of this book. Thank you to all my teachers and to my students, who have given me an opportunity to work through some of these ideas in the classroom.

Key names

Asaṅga: Legendary founder of the Buddhist Mahāyāna school called Yogācāra (also called Cittamātra or Mind-Only due to its supposed idealism). Author-editor of the *Yogācārabhūmiśāstra*, *c.* fourth to fifth century CE.

Bhartṛhari: Hindu philosopher of language, grammarian and author of the *Vākyapadīya*, *c.* fifth century.

Buddhamitra: A teacher of Vasubandhu and who may have been involved in debates with Sāṃkhyas that played a role in the development of the *Pātañjalayogaśāstra* (see Larson and Bhattacharya 2008: 41–2).

Dharmakīrti: Buddhist Mādhyamaka philosopher, who elaborates ideas of yogic perception (*yogipratyakṣa*) in the *Pramāṇavārttika*, *c.* seventh century.

Dharmatrāta, Ghoṣaka, Vasumitra, Buddhadeva: Four founding Buddhist scholar-monks in the Sarvāstivāda Abhidharma tradition, often referenced as a group in the early literature.

Dignāga: Buddhist logician. Author of *Pramāṇasamuccaya*, *c.* fifth to sixth century CE.

Īśvarakṛṣṇa: Author of the surviving foundational text of Sāṃkhya, the *Sāṃkhyakārikā*, *c.* fourth century CE.

Pañcaśikha: Traditionally a Sāṃkhya philosopher, sometimes attributed as the author of the lost *Ṣaṣṭitantra*. In the *Mahābhārata* known as the teacher of the King Janaka, *c.* first to second century CE.

Patañjali: Grammarian and author of the grammar treatise *Mahābhāṣya*, *c.* second century BCE, which is a commentary on Pāṇini's foundational *Aṣṭādhyāyī*, composed in *c.* sixth to fourth century BCE.

Patañjali: Author-editor of the *Yogasūtra* and possibly of the first surviving commentary (both works, when bundled together, are referred to as the *Pātañjalayogaśāstra*), *c.* second to fifth century CE.

Śaṅkara: Key figure in the nondual school of Vedānta (Advaita Vedānta). Flourished *c.* eighth century CE.

Vārṣagaṇya: Attributed author of a lost Sāṃkhya treatise called the *Ṣaṣṭitantra*, *c.* second century CE.

Vindhyavāsin: A Sāṃkhya author whom some scholars speculate may have had a role in composing the first commentary to the *Yogasūtra*, *c.* fourth to fifth century.

Vyāsa: Name attributed to author of first commentary on the *Yogasūtra*, by scholars who do not subscribe to the theory of an auto-commentary by Patañjali. Vyāsa also means 'editor' or 'arranger'.

Abbreviations

BG	*Bhagavad Gītā*
MBh	*Mahābhārata*
MuU	*Muṇḍaka Upaniṣad*
PYŚ	*Pātañjalayogaśāstra*
SvU	*Śvetāśvatara Upaniṣad*
TvS	*Tattvārthasūtra*
YS	*Yogasūtra*
YBh	*Yogasūtrabhāṣya*

Note on translations of *Pātañjalayogaśāstra*

Unless otherwise stated, all translations from the *Pātañjalayogaśāstra* are by the author and reference the Āgāśe 1904 critical edition. The *sūtra*s are shown in **bold** and the commentary in non-bold. If a quoted passage is from the *Yogasūtra* only, it will be referenced with the abbreviation YS and shown in bold. If a quoted passage is solely from or contains material from the commentary, it will be referenced with the abbreviation PYŚ (and any embedded *sūtra*s therein will be shown in bold).

Series editor preface

The introductions we include in the World Philosophies series take a single thinker, theme or text and provide a close reading of them. What defines the series is that these are likely to be people or traditions that you have not yet encountered in your study of philosophy. By choosing to include them you broaden your understanding of ideas about the self, knowledge and the world around us. Each book presents unexplored pathways into the study of world philosophies. Instead of privileging a single philosophical approach as the basis of comparison, each book accommodates the many different dimensions of cross-cultural philosophizing. While the choice of terms used by the individual volumes may indeed carry a local inflection, they encourage critical thinking about philosophical plurality. Each book strikes a balance between locality and globality.

In *The Philosophy of the Yogasūtra*, Karen O'Brien-Kop presents the *Yogasūtra* as a systematic philosophical text by decentering conventional readings that either perceive the *Yogasūtra* to be merely a manual for the bodily practice of yoga or continue to reproduce the hegemony of the philosophical universal. Through this approach, O'Brien-Kop familiarizes the reader with an intriguing worldview that bears on metaphysical, ontological, ethical and aesthetic issues even today.

1

Introduction: The context of the *Yogasūtra*

Chapter outline

Introduction

The *Yogasūtra* is a renowned text, not only in South Asia, where it is venerated as an important Hindu *sūtra* text (a condensed treatise) that imparts a philosophical system called 'yoga', but also around the world today where, in translation, it has become the foundational primary source for many different yoga communities. But how well do we read this text in the contemporary world? By 'well', I mean the willingness to engage with the spirit of the text as a *sūtra* and with its profundity and complexity as a philosophical work. These intrinsic facets of Patañjali's work are sometimes overlooked by contemporary readers, be they in Delhi or Los Angeles. The text is well known for a particular section called the *aṣṭāṅga* (eightfold) portion, which describes eight auxiliaries of yoga, more or less construed as a system of practice or sometimes as a 'practical philosophy'. However, this book seeks to encourage an integrated reading of Patañjali's work that takes the whole of the material into account and not just the portion that has proved most popular over history. As a philosophical treatise produced in the South Asian genre of the *sūtra*, Patañjali's text follows a standard and compact formula to express the scope, principles and depth of a tradition of enquiry that is underpinned by both abstract and embodied rationality.

Of course, the 'yoga' discussed in the *Yogasūtra* does relate to the contemporary phenomenon that bears the same name, but as a formal school or intellectual identity of philosophy Patañjali's text also expresses metaphysics, ontology, epistemology and logic as conceptualized, practised and argued in the early common era. Indeed, we can find here all the fundamental questions and answers of philosophy: What does it mean to be human? Can we live our lives ethically? What is the nature of consciousness? How can we attain freedom? What happens after death? How did the world begin? This book seeks to highlight and dive into the deeply inquisitive veins of rational exposition offered by the *Yogasūtra* as a worldview and as a practical philosophy. The enduring popularity of this text for some two millennia is testimony to the fact that it is not a historical relic, but represents a system of living, breathing philosophy, practised the world over by Hindus and by yoga practitioners of all religious, secular and cultural stripes.

This book also proposes that we go yet further in our assessment of the text – to push the *Yogasūtra* into the spotlight as a work that academic philosophers the world over should notice and include in their philosophy curricula. This is not only because of the inherent value of the text as a work of systematic philosophy, but also as a contribution to the decolonial project of globalizing philosophy. Hence, Patañjali can sit alongside Plato and Parmenides as a go-to philosopher of the ancient world who has something enduring to teach us about the self, virtue, the mind, reality or a myriad of other topics in human experience. This is a constructive counterview to a recent hysterical narrative about sidelining Plato (*Daily Mail* 2017)[1] and seeks an understanding of the history of rational enquiry in a way that is more accurate, representative and culturally wide-ranging. In short, the project of globalizing philosophy advocates for a 'pluriverse' rather than a 'universe' of thought (Mbembe 2016). Moreover, Patañjali's text has a particular valence for our times, be it in how the ethics of non-harm informs environmental activism and veganism, how care of the self (*à la* Foucault) is an instrument of ontological preservation in the political fight for social justice, in discussions of whether consciousness can be preserved in artificial intelligence (AI), in public policy on how to achieve better mental health through meditation, or in how a pared-back lifestyle disrupts the machinery of consumer capitalism. Because it is a systematic treatise, the questions addressed by Patañjali are extraordinarily wide-ranging and can speak to broad audiences today – both academic and non-academic – beyond those who perform yoga postures on a mat.

The *Yogasūtra* also has much to impart on reasoning, argumentation, aesthetics and philosophy of language. Indeed, the scope of philosophical topics is formidable given the brevity of the text. This very conciseness has, I believe, been part of the success of its transmission and translation over the ages. And yet this succinctness has also created a barrier of sorts to accessing the breadth and depth of ideas in the text. *Sūtra*s (aphorisms) are designed for mnemonic learning, but behind this surface pithiness is a deep cavern of ideas. Hence, we will read the *sūtra*s alongside the earliest extant commentary – variously thought to be an auto-commentary by Patañjali or a separate commentary by Vyāsa authored a century or so after the *sūtra*s. In any case, *sūtra*s were not designed to be digested as standalone pronouncements, but to act as gateways into larger bodies of teaching – traditionally expanded by a *guru* (teacher) or a scholastic commentator. And so, to really open up the range of philosophical discussions within the *Yogasūtra*, this book will also rely on the first commentary and, occasionally, the meandering, creative interpretations of later commentaries, simply because these traditional philosophical expositions are helpful (and sometimes essential) to understand the point at stake.

This book has employed the traditional branches of western philosophy to organize chapters and to make explicit the degree to which the content of the *Yogasūtra* addresses what is commonly studied as 'philosophy' in the western academy. While acknowledging the limits of employing western categories of philosophy in a project that seeks to contribute to decolonizing the discipline, the rationale is as follows: (a) Studies that explore the *Yogasūtra* as philosophy are often confined to metaphysics, ontology and ethics. By also drawing our attention to epistemology, logic, aesthetics and philosophy of language, these chapters demonstrate the depth and breadth of philosophical topics encompassed in Patañjali's system (beyond popular ideas of the text as a kind of 'practice manual'), (b) As this book is aimed at general academic readers, it is not assumed that readers will have full capacity to engage with the advanced and expert dimensions of Early Indian Philosophy (which requires a thorough grounding in its own right), and so the chapter titles offer familiar points of access for any student of philosophy, (c) A core aim of this book is to get Patañjali's work added to academic philosophy syllabi as a standard work, and one way to demonstrate the ease and value of reading the *Yogasūtra* as an important philosophical text is to show how it relates to existing areas of study on a philosophy programme (such as logic, ethics or philosophy of language). Above all, this book is intended to inspire students to read further. The discussion questions and introductory reading lists attached to each chapter are designed to initiate curiosity and to provide leads into deeper study of Indian philosophy as a whole and on its own terms.

Early systems of Indian philosophy: *Śāstra*s, *sūtra*s and 'schools'

The period from 500 BCE onwards was a time when South Asian thought was starting to be formally codified in comprehensive *śāstra*s (treatises)[2] and soon thereafter in the form of *sūtra*s (aphorisms), which were collected, organized and sequenced so as to represent a systematized worldview. When later Hindu doxographers[3] looked back on the period 500 BCE to 500 CE (often called the 'classical period'), they identified distinct streams or schools of thought, which, according to their historical lens could be grouped into Hindu and non-Hindu camps. The Hindu identities were organised as six 'schools'[4] and deemed *āstika* (lit. 'one who adheres to the Vedas'): Vaiśeiṣika, Mīmāṃsā, Vedānta, Nyāya, Sāṃkhya and Yoga (see Table 1). These school identities were structured around a recognizable format of a root text (in a *sūtra* style)[5] with subsequent authoritative commentary explanations. Other schools, which fell neither under the heading of 'Hindu thought' nor adhered to the concise *sūtra* format, were included under the rubric of 'heterodox' thought, *nāśtika* (lit. 'one who does not adhere to the Vedas'). This category included many Buddhist and Jain streams of philosophy.

Additionally, the *āstika* philosophical systems were paired as follows:

- Nyāya-Vaiśeṣika (both concerned with logical analysis – of arguments or atoms)
- Mīmāṃsā-Vedānta (both concerned with exegesis of the Vedic texts)
- Sāṃkhya-Yoga (both concerned with consciousness and rational reflection on ontology)

As we can see from the approximate chronology of philosophical *sūtra*s – shown in Table 1 – the *Yogasūtra* (whether we date it to fourth century CE,

Table 1 Traditional scheme of early Hindu systems of philosophy (by estimated chronology). © Karen O'Brien-Kop.

System of thought	Root text	Attributed author	Approximate dating
Vaiśeṣika	*Vaiśeṣikasūtra*	Kaṇāda	*c.* 3rd–2nd century BCE
Mīmāṃsā	*Mīmāṃsāsūtra*	Jaimini	*c.* 2nd century BCE
Vedānta[6]	*Brahmasūtra*	Bādarāyana	*c.* 2nd century BCE–2nd century CE
Nyāya	*Nyāyasūtra*	Gautama	*c.* 2nd–3rd century CE
Sāṃkhya	*Sāṃkhyakārikā*	Īśvarakṛṣṇa	*c.* 4th century CE
Yoga	*Yogasūtra*	Patañjali	*c.* 4th–5th century CE

or earlier)[7] appears towards the end of this formative period in systematic philosophy. The text therefore takes much that was discussed in the other schools for granted, and so by reading the *Yogasūtra* we are engaging not just with the philosophy of 'yoga', but also finding out about precepts, ideas and worldviews of, for example, Sāṃkhya, Vaiśeṣika and Nyāya philosophy (as well as Jain and Buddhist thought, discussed below).

Of course 'philosophy' as an anglophone term is but an approximation for the many technical Sanskrit terms that we encounter to indicate reasoning and argumentation in Indian thought. The most prevalent term used is *darśana* (lit. 'seeing'), the first use of which is sometimes traced to the *Vaiśeṣikasūtra* (9.2.13) of Kaṇāda, where it may indicate something like 'body of knowledge'.[8] *Darśana* means 'seeing' or 'becoming visible' and indicates a deep anchoring of Indian philosophy in 'perception', as evident in the centrality to all the systems of ocular-centric terms and goals such as viewpoint, insight or vision of truth (linked back to the 'seers' or poet-sages of the Vedic tradition, the *ṛṣis*). However, there are also many other technical terms that point to what we might translate as 'philosophy', including *ānvīkṣikī* (method of logic), *tarkaśāstra* (method of reasoning), *mata* (belief), *nyāya* (logic), *siddhānta* (conclusion or position), *tantra* (framework or system), *tattvajñāna* (knowledge of the constituents [of reality]), *vāda* (doctrine), and *vidyā* (knowledge) (Aklujkar 2017; Halbfass 1988: 263–86).

The *Yogasūtra* of Patañjali was composed against a backdrop of social, political and cultural change in South Asia. The period of approximately 200 BCE to 300 CE was one that is sometimes called 'between the empires' (i.e. after the fall of the Mauryan empire but before the consolidation of Gupta rule).[9] During this time there was political disquiet and a shift in hegemonic thought from Buddhism to Brahmanism across the subcontinent, forming the basis for the establishment of a Hindu episteme as the dominant paradigm by the fourth century (Olivelle 2006; Sathaye 2022). However, Patañjali does not write about collective political freedom, but rather the freedom of the existential subject. The text instructs on how to cultivate a lifestyle that is ethically based, oriented to asceticism and focused on discipline in order to acquire stillness, clarity and insight in the mental sphere (more or less within the confines of normative Brahmanical identity). Indeed, the end goal of the text promises knowledge of the self, such that there is a radical identification with consciousness over materiality to the degree that an ultimate state of isolated consciousness can be attained – a state labelled freedom.

This ideal of freedom, however, should be understood in the broader cultural context of the time, constituted not only by Brahmanical philosophical investigation, but also by Buddhist and Jain. All three groups adhered to an analysis of the human condition as associated with chronic existential dis-ease, categorized variously as 'suffering' (*duḥkha*) or 'pain/distress' (*tapa*). Moreover, these worldviews commonly located the fundamental problem as an error in the perception of the self and hence also of the world. Each of the Brahmanical schools and sub-schools offers a unique analysis of self-misperception, but the basic shared idea is that the self (*ātman*) is permanent and unchanging beneath the vagaries of personality and daily life. For the Buddhists, the key error was to perceive the self as permanent when it was, in fact, in a state of constant flux and without any fixed essence (*anātman*). The Jains, like the Brahmins, held to the notion of a pure and fixed self (*jīva*), restricted by an embodied scaffolding of delusion, veiled perception and existential bondage. Equally, all three communities subscribed to an ethical theory of action (*karma*), whereby the nature of self was informed and shaped not only by actions in this lifetime but also in past lifetimes, the sum total of which determined the recurrence of birth into future lifetimes. Until residues of past actions could be eliminated (via ascetic practices of purification) and a state of perfect moral virtue attained, individuals would be bound to the wheel of rebirth (*saṃsāra*). Each school – whether *āstika* or *nāstika* – combined abstract philosophical reasoning with practical and embodied philosophy as a means to an acute end: the freedom of the self. This freedom was variously called *mokṣa* (liberation/emancipation) in Hinduism and Jainism, *bodhi* (awakened) in Buddhism and Jainism, and *nirvāṇa* (cessative liberation) in Buddhism.

Archaic meanings of 'yoga'

A word on 'yoga'. The term 'yoga' as encountered in Patañjali's treatise bears many denotations and connotations that are resonant with contemporary understandings of the term. ('Yoga' is now a borrowed word in English and many other languages.) However, the Sanskrit word *yoga* also had specific meanings in its own time and context, and we shall endeavour to adhere closely, where necessary, to those fourth-century understandings. Although the word *yoga* appears in the Vedas[10] with generic (and often prosaic) meanings linked to 'joining' and 'conjoining', by the last section of the Vedic canon, the Upaniṣads, the term emerges with a more specific religio-philosophical meaning of contemplative and ascetic means to know the nature of the self (*ātmatattva*) (SvUp 2.15). At the same time as the meaning of *yoga* was crystallizing in Brahmanical contexts such as the epic *Mahābhārata* (including the *Bhagavad Gītā*), other philosophical groups had their own understandings. The Jains defined *yoga* as 'connection' in order to indicate the weight of karmic deposit that attached to and entrapped the individuated self (*jīvātman*).[11] Buddhists developed specific understandings of *yogācāra* (discipline of *yoga*)[12] as meditation practice in the Buddhist vein (discussed below). In the formation of the philosophical canon of *sūtra* texts listed above, *yoga* is discussed relatively infrequently, indicating its slightly later entry to the canon and that it was not necessarily a highly visible conversation partner in this forum. However, by adopting the metaphysics of Sāṃkhya, a school that saturated the ancient philosophical disputes, Patañjali announced that *yoga*, although an archaic concept and contemplative practice, now had something innovative and distinct to contribute to this body of *formal* philosophical knowledge.

In Sāṃkhya, the methods proposed are more abstract than Pātañjala yoga, in that they are focused solely on rational reflection, namely deep contemplation of each constituent of reality (*tattva*) and how it sits in relation to other constituents. However, Sāṃkhya also relies on argumentation and reasoning to demonstrate conclusive proof of the true nature of reality. Pātañjala yoga adopted this system of reasoning and combined it with the more intuitive contemplative methods of the Upaniṣads, the structured meditation techniques of Buddhism, an ethical code and some vestiges of the embodied practices of asceticism. In yoga, the preparation for rational reflection is a long-term commitment, and since it incorporates practical ethics and the development of physical purity and fitness for sustained meditation, it can require a lifetime's engagement.[13]

An overview of the *Yogasūtra*

The *Yogasūtra* was composed around the second century to fourth CE with current approximations for the final redaction as the fourth to fifth century CE. Certainly, parts of the text may have been older and in circulation for centuries before this, but analysis of how the text relates intertextually to other works (particularly Buddhist texts) suggests that it crystallized in its preserved form during the fourth or fifth century (Maas 2013, 2020). Authorship is attributed to 'Patañjali', which was already an authoritative name in scholastic circles since the time of the renowned grammarian Patañjali, who wrote a treatise called the *Mahābhāṣya* in the second century BCE. The two figures are clearly separate. What is unclear, however, is whether the *Yogasūtra* was the work of one 'author' or, more likely, several composers and editors over some centuries, all grouped under the name 'Patañjali'. Hence, the text is most likely a combination of traditional and ancient material with new and original composition, put together in the fourth century. As mentioned above, the *Yogasūtra* can be regarded as a standalone composition by Patañjali or a combined text containing a commentary also by Patañjali (and hence an 'auto-commentary'), with both texts together called the *Pātañjalayogaśāstra*.[14] There are differing views in scholarship as to whether this commentary should be attributed to Patañjali or to a later author called Vyāsa, but for the purpose of this study, we will not consider such philological scholarship but simply propose the value of reading both texts together in order to better understand the philosophical scope and objectives of the *Yogasūtra*.

Outline of content

The *Yogasūtra* of Patañjali is composed of 195 *sūtra*s (aphorisms)[15] and divided into four *pāda*s (chapters). It bears instructions on a philosophical system called 'yoga', which on the whole deals with conceptual abstractions. Yet the text also outlines preparatory embodied practices as a means to access the deeper rationality of the system.

The best known maxim of the *Yogasūtra* is *yogaś cittavṛttinirodhaḥ* (YS 1.2), 'yoga is the cessation of the fluctuations of the mind', i.e. the cessation of thought processes. Soon after this opening statement, the text proposes practice (*abhyāsa*) and dispassion (*vairāgya*) as the two primary means to achieve this cessation. Patañjali's first chapter focuses on forms of mental concentration (*samādhi*), based on either cognitive or non-cognitive techniques. The second chapter describes an active method (*kriyā yoga*) composed of three techniques: austerity (*tapas*), Vedic recitation (*svādhyāya*)[16] and contemplation on īśvara (the lord, a higher principle or being that is ambivalently theisized). This method is designed to reduce or eliminate the negative states of mind called the *kleśa*s, or 'afflictions', in order to attain *samādhi* (concentration). Next comes another method, that of *aṣṭāṅga yoga*, or the yoga of eight auxiliaries. This account is spread across Chapters 2 and 3:

1. *yama* (ethical restraints) (YS 2.30–31)
   These restraints are social or relational: *ahiṃsā* (non-harm), *satya* (truth), *asteya* (non-stealing), *brahmacārya* (celibacy/continence), *aparigraha* (non-grasping).

2. *niyama* (ethical observances) (YS 2.40–45)
   These observances are about self-discipline: *śauca* (purity/cleanliness), *saṃtoṣa* (contentedness), *tapas* (austerity), *svādhyāya* (recitation or study of scripture), *īśvarapraṇidhāna* (contemplation on *īśvara*).

3. *āsana* (seat/posture) (YS 2.46–48)
   Āsana means sitting, abiding or seat. *Āsana* here indicates a seat for meditation, and we are told that this sitting posture should be steady and comfortable.

4. *prāṇāyāma* (breath-control) (YS 2.49–52)
   This technique entails regulating the breath and practising suspension of breath after inbreath or outbreath. There are various ways of measuring the breath.

5. *pratyāhāra* (sense withdrawal) (YS 2.53–55)
   The sense capacities are withdrawn from the everyday world, which facilitates utmost control of the senses, detachment from the material world, and higher sense perception.

6. *dhāraṇā* (mental fixing) (YS 3.1)
   The individual is now ready to proceed with the three states of meditation. The mind is fixed or bound to a single object of focus. Such foci can be internal, such as the navel point, the heart, the head, the tip of the nose, the tip of the tongue. Foci can also be external objects.

7. *dhyāna* (absorption) (YS 3.2)
   The fixing of the mind is extended through time to become steady and uninterrupted. The mind enters a state in which there is no disturbance to the focus and in which a directed stream of attention flows.

8. *samādhi* (perfected concentration) (YS 3.3)
   In this perfected concentration, perception becomes crystal-clear and one-pointed, facilitating the highest levels of realization.

The next section is a list of the special faculties obtained by consciousness undergoing transformation during *samādhi*. These special faculties are called *siddhi*s (perfections, attainments). Such *siddhi*s can contain special forms of knowledge about the cosmos as well as the supernatural attainments of invisibility, atomization, possession of other minds and superhuman strength.[17] The last chapter explains in more detail the nature of the goal of yoga. This goal is ontological and epistemological isolation, *kaivalya*, the separation of the categories of materiality and consciousness (*prakṛti* and *puruṣa*), revealing the Sāṃkhya frame of the method. This realization of consciousness is the state of liberation, and it follows from the capacity for discriminating discernment (*vivekakhyāti*). This refers to the ability to both know the difference between consciousness and materiality, and to exist as that difference: when one realizes that one's true nature is consciousness alone, then one attains spiritual liberation. Another means of realization is *pratiprasava*, a key technique from Sāṃkhya. *Pratiprasava* means dissolution or involution, the inverse of the process of the emanation of material reality. In terms of individual practice, then, *pratiprasava* entails the gradual withdrawal of the senses from the everyday world during meditation to the point where the practitioner starts to dissociate from the conventions of material existence – the identification with the body, the social self, one's environment, even time and space. Only in this state of splendid isolation, *kaivalya*, can one begin to witness from the non-engaged standpoint of pure consciousness (*puruṣa*). It is here that one can rest, supremely aware that the true self is eternal and unchanging consciousness, and therefore ultimately unaffected by the vagaries of everyday life, mental afflictions and suffering itself.

The three methods and epistemology

In the reception history of the text, both within and outside South Asia, the method that has been most focused on is that of an eight-staged formula (*aṣṭāṅga yoga*). However, the text delineates three different ways to attain the goal of yoga: concentration (*samādhi*), action (*kriyā*) and a method that mixes the two (i.e. the eightfold method, *aṣṭāṅga*). At the beginning of the second *pāda* (chapter), we are told by Patañjali that he has so far described concentrative techniques for one who knows how to control the mind (*citta*), through cognitive and non-cognitive means (*saṃprajñāta* and *asaṃprajñāta*). The same passage then announces that the second *pāda* will focus on methods for adepts who are still engaged with the world and its fluctuations:

> Yoga of the concentrated mind (*samāhitacitta*) has been described. How then might one whose mind is agitated (*vyutthitacitta*) be established in yoga (*yogayukta*)?
>
> (PYŚ 2.1)

The text proceeds to explain two approaches that are more accessible: the method of action (*kriyā yoga*) and the method of eight stages or auxiliaries (*aṣṭāṅga yoga*)[18] (this exposition continues over the second and third *pādas*). For each of these three primary methods (concentration, action and eight stages) the text indicates that, as in Buddhist and Jain systems of meditation, contemplative practices are designed for sequential attainment. Hence one stage (*bhūmi*) builds progressively on the completion of another (PYŚ 3.6) and the text's varied formulas of contemplation, reflection or embodied practice are sequential in design, much like systems of reasoning.

Indeed, Patañjali's first chapter establishes a connection between formal epistemology and these three ways to attain 'the highest yoga' (*yoga uttamam*):

> Thus it is said: 'By means of scripture (*āgama*), inference (*anumāṇa*), and by the essence of the practice (*abhyāsa*) of [mental] absorption (*dhyāna*), by these three, one ascertains insight (*prajñā*) and ascertains the highest yoga (*yogam uttamam*)'.
>
> (PYŚ 1.48)

These 'three means' refer to the three valid bases of knowledge or *pramāṇas* – authority, perception and inference – which loosely correlate to the three yogic methods of the *Yogasūtra* (see also 'Chapter 4: Epistemology'). So, authority (or scripture) is associated with *kriyā yoga* (in its practice of Vedic recitation and near-theism), and perception is associated with the concentrative meditation called *samādhi* (both cognitive and non-cognitive). Right perception is also highlighted as the goal of the eight auxiliaries. So where does inference fit in? Inference is the process of reasoning that pervades the rational reflection called concentration. Patañjali's yoga is not an affective method that entails 'bliss' or 'rapture', but rather proposes steady, regulated and reasoned reflection on the nature of reality. Hence, inference is the unravelling of subtle causal effects as made visible through the constituents of reality (*tattvas*). The inferential process leads one back to the 'source' of the material world (*mūlaprakṛti*), a ground of material dissolution that we might call primordial matter. Taken from Sāṃkhya ontological contemplation (see also 'Chapter 2: Metaphysics: The world and reality'),[19] these inferential processes are designed to lead one to true apprehension of reality and are at the heart of concentrative meditation in the *Yogasūtra*. By aligning the methods of 'yoga' to these three valid bases of knowledge, Patañjali not only situates his text among the recognized schools of philosophy, but demonstrates that these yoga methods are valid means to reach true conclusions.

Buddhist and Jain worldviews

So far, we have situated the *Pātañjalayogaśāstra* as a religio-philosophical text with extraordinary longevity and impact into present times. We have contextualized the text in the formal philosophical milieu in which it was forged, that of the *darśanas* or systematic philosophy, and we have noted its particular reliance on a school of thought called Sāṃkhya. However, it is also important to acknowledge the deep imbrication of Patañjali's treatise with the philosophical systems of Buddhism and Jainism.

While the Upaniṣads innovated many new ideas and questions around ontology, ethics, epistemology and soteriology (such as theories of reality, self, action and liberating knowledge), it is difficult to extricate these new concepts from those that were developing in adjacent non-Vedic cultures during the same period. Although Vedic culture was established in the northwest of India, it gradually moved eastwards, where it encountered new renunciant (*śramaṇa*) movements growing up around the area east of the Gangetic Plain, sometimes referred to as the Greater Magadha region (Bronkhorst 2007). A *śramaṇa* is one who performs acts of austerity, and this epithet is derived from the verbal root √*śram*, meaning 'to strive, to exert'. (It is also from this verb that we derive the more familiar term ashram or *āśram*, 'a place of rest'.) The *śramaṇa* movements grew up in the sixth to fifth century BCE and included new groups such as the Ājīvikas (led by Maskarin Gosāla), the Jains (led by Vardamāna Mahāvīra) and the Buddhists (led by Gautama Buddha). These ascetic groups crucially explored the idea that suffering is born from activity, and proposed that one must abstain from activity by disengaging from society and conventional comforts. Jain ascetic practices could include standing in the sun for days on end, or fasting for long periods. Other key Jain ideas were those of non-harm (*ahiṃsā*) and of committing to 'great vows' or ethical observances (*mahāvratas*). Buddhism eschewed extreme asceticism and focused on desire as the basis of suffering. It is likely that, through contact, there was some form of conceptual sharing between Brahmins and these groups on the issues of transmigration and liberation.

One of the most important Jain texts to discuss yoga was the *c.* fifth-century *Tattvārthasūtra*. This text was written by Umāsvāti and was the first Jain text to be written in Sanskrit (rather than the vernacular Prakrit). It occupies a similar status in Śvetāmbara Jainism[20] to the *Yogasūtra* in Hinduism and is regarded as an exemplar of classical Jain philosophy. In the *Tattvārthasūtra,* cyclic existence *(saṃsāra)* was understood as threefold: body, speech and mind. This threefold mundane activity was called *yoga*:

> *Yoga* is the action (*karma*) of body, speech and mind.
>
> (TvS 6.1)[21]

Furthermore, yoga was the capacity of the soul to bind karma to itself – karmic repercussion was defined as a substance (or particles) that stuck to the pure self (*jīva*). The aim of Jain practice was to attain the path of liberation (*mokṣamārga*), and this was brought about through *yoganirodha*, the cessation of activity (*yoga*) that produces *karma*. We can see that the aims of Pātañjala yoga and Jain ascetic practice were broadly similar in that they shared the idea of a permanent self (unlike the Buddhists) and sought an end goal of cessation (*nirodha*) by putting a stop to karmic activity. Umāsvāti's goal of *cittanirodha* (the end of the mind) echoes Patañjali's *cittavṛttinirodha* (the end of mental flux).

There has been a good deal of scholarship on the presence of Buddhist ideas in the *Yogasūtra*. (For a recent roundup, see O'Brien-Kop 2021: 2–7.) A particularly interesting case in point is the community of ascetic Buddhist monks who cultivated *yogācāra* (the discipline of yoga) in the early centuries of the first millennium. *Yogācāra* consisted of techniques of meditation and austere living in order to attain liberation (*nirvāṇa*). Like the yogins, the *yogācāra*s were advanced practitioners of meditation. They spent long periods in retreat in isolated conditions (generally known as 'forest-dwelling') and were sometimes perceived to have extraordinary capacities (*siddhi*s). The early Buddhist Mahāyāna *sūtras* laid out different systems of meditation that lead to distinct levels of concentration (*samādhi*s). The precise religious and philosophical affiliations of these early *yogācāra*s are still uncertain because much of their literature is lost to history. However, by the fifth century CE this community had grown in significance and eventually consolidated as a community of philosophers in the Mahāyāna stream of Buddhism. The knowledge of *yogācāra* was codified by Asaṅga in the voluminous compendium *Yogācārabhūmiśāstra*. The *Yogācārabhūmiśāstra* (*The Treatise on the Foundations of Yoga Discipline*) systematized information about meditation practices that led to liberation. These included practices of meditative cultivation (*bhāvanā*) in order to eliminate one's mental afflictions (*kleśa*s) and to achieve the status of a *bodhisattva* (one who has taken a vow towards liberation). While *yogācāra* texts provided detailed explanations of the mind and meditation, the descriptions of posture (*āsana*) were limited to simple static poses that could facilitate long periods of meditation.

Another important strand of Buddhist thought was that of Abhidharma, which concentrated on developing taxonomies of the constituents of material reality, the parts or building blocks of which were called *dharmas*. Buddhist Ābhidharmikas created categories for everything that existed and suggested meditative practices that could yield knowledge of these categories. We also find detailed classification of universal reality in Sāṃkhya philosophy in the system of the *tattvas* (the elements or levels of reality) (see 'Chapter 2. Metaphysics: The world and reality'). Given that the Sāṃkhya and Ābhidharmika systems of philosophy flourished alongside each other in the early common era, we can infer that some form of conceptual sharing occurred. Patañjali adheres to the Sāṃkhya system of the *tattvas*, but, on occasion, he also mentions *dharmas* in an ambiguous sense, and this may relate to the Abhidharma context. Scholars have shown that there are some instances of closely related wording between the *Yogasūtra*, its commentary and the Buddhist author Vasubandhu's *Abhidharmakośabhāṣya*. Again, this suggests that authors such as Patañjali and Vasubandhu had some knowledge of each other's systems of thought (Maas 2020; O'Brien-Kop 2018).

Epistemic frames

Finally, the hermeneutic approach of this book is, as much as possible, to explore and explain the worldview laid out by Patañjali in the *circa* fourth century, while also understanding and highlighting its continued relevance to our times and lives. An episteme is a principled system of knowledge – like a frame through which we view and understand the world. Societies or cultures at certain points in history have shared an episteme, built on certain assumptions about values and reality. Privileging Patañjali's episteme may sometimes require us to bracket our own, modern assumptions. As Ranganathan states, to truly understand the *Yogasūtra* as a work of philosophy we need to abandon 'naturalism and empiricism in favor of nonnaturalism and yoga rationalism (*jñāna*-ism)' (Ranganathan 2017: 178). His argument here is that modern Eurocentric categories such as 'naturalism' (the world can be fully explained by science) and 'empiricism' (valid knowledge comes from the senses) are limited or even redundant in the South Asian episteme, which has its own modes and bases of knowledge. There are reductive dangers of translating philosophical categories and terms across cultures, and Ranganathan points out that in the slippage of epistemic frames (a process that he calls interpretation), the reader can fail to notice that there are 'competing theories' between terms such as '*dharma*' and 'ethics', or between '*mokṣa*' and 'freedom' (Ranganathan 2017: 180). Hence we should play close attention to the internal logic and dynamics of Patañjali's systematized worldview.

Ranganathan proposes a reading strategy that he calls 'explication', which recognizes that translation in itself does not guarantee 'accuracy' of the objective meaning of the source text, and that a text may be imprecisely translated but relatively truthful to the original philosophy. While this method runs into problems regarding its presupposition that a text's 'original' meaning can be recovered, there is an important point here about the nature of *śāstra* – that it was designed as a system for objective transmission of truths. While individual interpretation did not enter into this process (for 'authors' or 'readers') there is merit in considering that there are some 'objective truths' to Patañjali's system because the text has resonated for different audiences over history, including those not familiar with the precise contexts of Indian philosophy or Sanskrit. Nonetheless, I have made every effort to produce translations of *sūtra*s and commentary passages that are as accurate as possible to the language and grammar of the Sanskrit expressions. Some scholars can be dismissive of the value of commentaries in understanding Patañjali's *sūtra*s, and I agree that even though the commentators believed that they were engaged in an objective explication, in reality they filtered the *sūtra*s through later epistemic lenses (often that of Vedānta). Yet if 'interpretation' is to be relied on, a historical South Asian interpretation (i.e. a commentary), no matter how flawed, is surely closer to the 'meanings' and cultural referents of Patañjali's text than a twenty-first-century globalized frame can yield.

What we shall discover in this book is that the *Yogasūtra* as a work of philosophy instructs us not only about its specific method for reaching consciousness-as-liberation (educating us in theories of mind, self, ethics and world), but is also a tapestry of philosophical methods, ideas, principles and frameworks from the age of the *sūtras* and *śāstras*. When read together with its first commentary, the *Yogasūtra* has much to impart about philosophy of language, logic and argumentation, aesthetics and epistemology. Finally, although it is a text of 'classical philosophy', we shall be treating this text not as a historical artefact, but as a living and breathing philosophy that is relevant to many millions of individuals around the world now.

Discussion questions

1. What are the different contexts of the word 'yoga' discussed in this chapter? Can a word retain a core meaning over several millennia? Does being a translated or borrowed word affect its meaning?
2. Which episteme informs your worldview? Does it affect how you approach this text?
3. What is the standing of Indian philosophy in western academic philosophy? What have been the historical barriers to more widespread and integrated reading of Indian philosophical texts outside of South Asia?

Further reading

Aklujkar, A. (2017) 'History and Doxography of the Philosophical Schools' in Ganeri, J. (ed.) *The Oxford Handbook of Indian Philosophy*. Oxford: Oxford University Press.

Chakravarthi, R. (2001) *Knowledge and Liberation in Classical Indian Thought*. Hampshire and New York: Palgrave Macmillan.

Ganeri, J. (2001) *Philosophy in Classical India: The Proper Work of Reason*. London and New York: Routledge.

Halbfass, W. (1988) '*Darśana, Ānvīkṣikī*, Philosophy' in *India and Europe: An Essay in Philosophical Understanding*. New York: SUNY.

Gupta, B. (2012) 'Introduction' in *An Introduction to Indian Philosophy: Perspectives on Reality, Knowledge and Freedom*. New York and Abingdon: Routledge.

Kirloskar-Steinbach, M. and Kalmanson, L. (2021) *A Practical Guide to World Philosophies: Selves, Worlds, and Ways of Knowing*. London and New York: Bloomsbury Academic.

Maldonado-Torres, N., Vizcano, V., Wallace, J. and We, J. E. A. (2018) 'Decolonizing Philosophy' in Bhambra, G. K., Gebrial, D. and Niancolu, K. (eds.) *Decolonizing the University*. London: Pluto Press.

Mohanty, J. N. (2000) *Classical Indian Philosophy*. Lanham: Rowman and Littlefield.

Sathaye, A. (2022) 'Introduction: A Cultural History of Hinduism in the Classical Age' in Sathaye, A. (ed.) *A Cultural History of Hinduism in the Classical Age (200BCE–800CE)*. London and New York: Bloomsbury Publishing.

2

Metaphysics: The world and reality

Chapter outline

The world

Patañjali offers an account of the world that largely adheres to the metaphysics of the Sāṃkhya system. Hence the world and reality are understood as permanent and eternal, partly underpinned by a substantial and temporal substratum that is fundamentally unchanging. Unlike the dominant Indian worldviews of the period – across Brahmanism, Buddhism and Jainism – the Sāṃkhya metaphysics was dualist. The world, then, is understood to be constituted by two aspects, materiality (*prakṛti*) and consciousness (*puruṣa*), which are each essential, but non-interacting. It is this fundamental and relatively streamlined understanding of reality on which we will focus in this chapter.

What is sometimes glossed over, however, are the traces of more archaic cosmologies in the text, such as the detailed cosmology laid out in the commentary to YS 3.26 in which seven worlds (*loka*s) are documented, ranged over three divisions of earth (including various hells), an intermediate atmospheric region (including the stars) and various invisible ascending heavenly regions. These heavenly realms are associated in ascending order with the gods Indra, Prajāpati and Brahmā and reflect the more archaic worldview of the Vedas. The extent of this cosmological worldview, with all of the different types of beings and topographies accounted for, is astonishing and poetic in its fine detail, and reflects the scholastic and textual heritage of the authors and editors of this *śāstra*. However, for the most part, such archaic worldviews are no more than descriptive flourishes in the text, which promotes a singular understanding of reality.

We can, perhaps, think of the world as the total environment or realm of possibility in which being dwells, although there may be a real or unreal apprehension of that world. Reality then is the true conception of, knowledge of and existence in the world as it is. So how does the world begin? There is no beginning point; rather the world (in its real and unreal dimensions) is understood as having existed eternally, without a specific beginning point. Hence the world is not engendered, but rather is a stable and continuously existing reality. Within this framework of eternalism, however, there are expressions of time, which take the form of cycles; these cycles are only real in the material domain of *prakṛti* and do not affect the domain of consciousness (*puruṣa*). Sāṃkhya metaphysics accounts for a material reality that is both changing and permanent through a mechanism that we can call emanation. Materiality exists in a base or primordial state of pure potentiality (*mūlaprakṛti*) – also referred to in Sāṃkhya-Yoga as *aliṅga* (without a mark), *avyakta* (unmanifest) and *pradhāna* (primordial) – until there is a stimulus that brings about a change in its state (which we cannot refer to as a cause – more on this below). Yet even when primordial reality dwells in pure stasis, it is still informed by three principles (*guṇa*s): dynamism (*rajas*), inertia (*tamas*) and balance (*sattva* – a word also used to express the notions of 'truth' and 'purity').

> *Sattva* has the character of light. *Rajas* has the character of action. *Tamas* has the character of fixity.
>
> (PYŚ 2.17)

Following a stimulus – which is best described as the proximal light of consciousness – the three principles move from stasis to engagement, which produces the evolutes of subjectivity and eventually of the world in its material expression. Since the first emanations are levels of the mind (see Figure 1), there is a sense in which the world evolves from mind. This continues a core theme of the Vedas, in which it is suggested that a divine mind exists and that only the mind of a sage (*ṛṣi*) can glimpse and understand truths that lie beyond the material realm. One of the best-known cosmogonical compositions of the *Ṛg Veda*, the 'Creation Hymn' or 'Nāsadīya', hints at a mind (*manas*) that is the source of the world, identical neither with being nor non-being (perhaps suggesting a transcendent mind):

> Desire came upon that one in the beginning; that was the first seed of the mind. Poets seeking in their heart with wisdom found the bond of existence in non-existence.
>
> (RV 10.129.4; trs. Doniger-O'Flaherty 1981: 25–6)

As evolutes continue to form and shape, initially through the mind and then through the embodied senses and elemental states, there is an unfolding of the material realm from subtle to gross dimensions. These emanations are summed up precisely in a taxonomy known as the 25 constituents (*tattva*s), as shown in Figure 1.

Because of the primacy of mind (be it universal or subjective) in this map of the emanations, there is a basis to argue that this understanding of reality is idealist, i.e. that reality or the experience thereof is in part or whole dependent on mental perception. Hence, Burley argues that what is connoted as *prakṛti* in Figure 1 is not materiality in the sense of the objective world, but rather a Kantian-style presentation of how human subjectivity mediates the contact with and processing

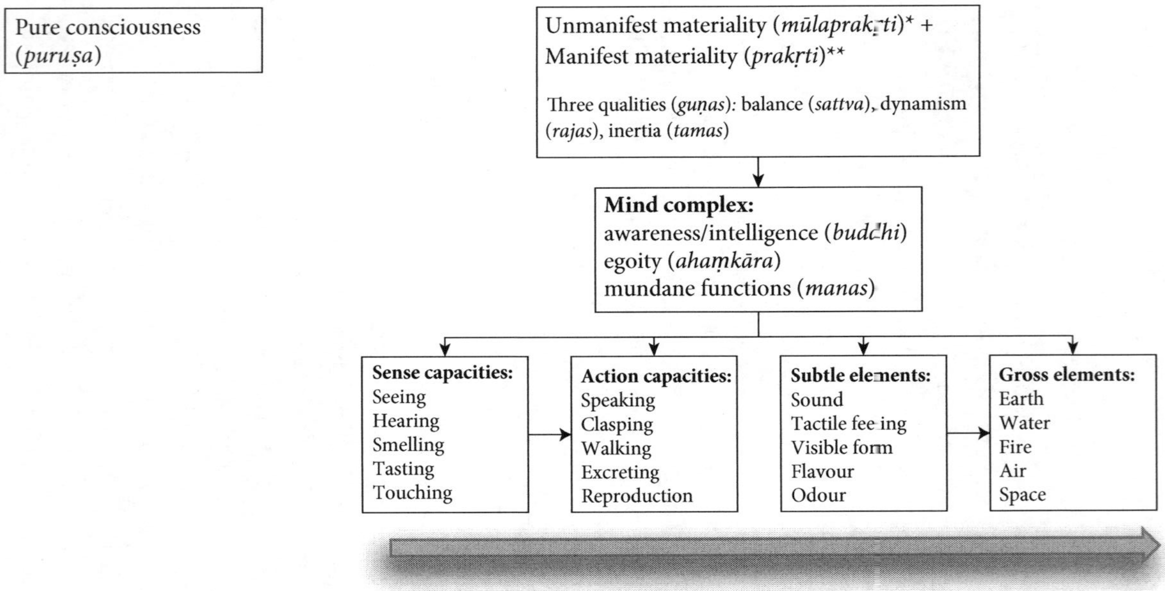

**mūlaprakṛti* (root or base materiality) is also called *pradhāna* (primordial), *aliṅga* (without a mark), and *avyakta* (unmanifest)

***prakṛti* (materiality) is also called *liṅga* (with a mark) and *vyakta* (manifest)

Figure 1 Sāṃkhya-Yoga dualist metaphysics: emanation. © Karen O'Brien-Kop.

of external reality (Burley 2007). For Burley, the Sāṃkhya taxonomy represents consciousness and subjectivity, but not objective materiality itself, which, he argues, is not addressed in this system.[1] Burley therefore presents the twenty-three evolutes of *prakṛti* as a set of transcendental conditions of possibility rather than an account of material causality in which gross elements such as air, fire, water, etc. emerge from subtle (mental) elements such as intelligence, egoity or mind. Ashton (2020) makes a related argument, by positing that the existential mix-up between *puruṣa* and *prakṛti* takes place not at a general metaphysical level, but rather specifically between *puruṣa* and *mūlaprakṛti* (primordial materiality). Somewhat in line with Burley (2007), Ashton argues that when viewed this way, the emanation of *prakṛti* refers not to the whole of material reality but to the particular instantiation of a human being and its experience of reality over one lifetime (an embodied existence that is fashioned from *mūlaprakṛti*).

I propose an understanding that can encompass both philosophical standpoints, i.e. that *prakṛti* refers to 'materiality', 'material objective world' or even 'principle of materiality' while also acknowledging that Burley's and Ashton's arguments for a centring of subjectivity over objectivity are compelling. So, let's posit that the emanations of *prakṛti* point to the array of substantial components of objective reality, including (but not limited to) the human embodied subject and beginning with this facet of reality (subjectivity) because it constitutes the standpoint from which we can start to 'know' the rest of material reality. These points will be discussed further in Chapters 3 and 4 of this book. For now, however, let's stay with the big picture of what reality consists of.

What is a dualist reality?

In the broadest terms, reality is, as Larson and Bhattacharya analysed (2008), co-fundamental and co-ultimate – neither materiality nor consciousness can be subtracted from reality, and neither principle supersedes the other. Indeed, although independent, both facets are necessary to make up the whole. The dualism is thus about irreconcilable difference, and the rational method proposed in Sāṃkhya and followed in Pātañjala yoga is about the perception of this difference (*vivekakhyāti*, or 'discriminating discernment'). The word *sāṃkhya* itself carries the meaning of 'enumeration' or 'counting'. This expresses the idea that knowing reality is to be able to accurately enumerate and describe its constituents, at the most basic level in the discrimination between consciousness and materiality and, in a more textured sense, to know the 25 constituents (*tattvas*) of reality, including all the complex material emanations (see Figure 1). This knowledge of the essential features of reality leads to apprehension of the true nature of the world – and how time, space, materiality and consciousness all function in relation. Many scholars have commented on the apparent equivalence in this dualist metaphysics – that consciousness and matter are separate but equal. However, there are two key points pertaining to this metaphysics that challenge this claim. The first is the clear privileging of knowledge over embodiment in the account of subjectivity (discussed next) and the second point is the way in which this dualist division is constructed through gendered concepts (discussed below).

The value and purpose of materiality and consciousness

The first point is that the ultimate vision of truth in this worldview identifies consciousness as the prime principle and not materiality. When the subject correctly perceives reality as dual, they also correctly perceive the true self as pure consciousness. While the material body is subject to decay in the material world (with each life cycle representing that very power of *prakṛti* to emanate and then dissolve), there is a deeper, unseen dimension to the self. This dimension, consciousness, is not part of the material world and is never subject to change or deterioration. In this sense, Sāṃkhya-Yoga offers us an understanding of an enduring part of the self that does not die. But it is not termed the *ātman* or self of Brahmanism, nor the *jīva* or soul/self of Jainism, nor, indeed, the *anātman* or non-self of Buddhism. Rather this is a theory of consciousness as a part of ourselves (the enduring part) that is termed *puruṣa*. In some sense, this connects to questions of a modern sensibility, such as 'is there life after death?', 'does consciousness die when the body dies?', 'is consciousness a property of the brain or the wider body?', 'can we download consciousness to AI' or 'can we preserve consciousness by cyrogenizing the body?' and so on. There is a distinctly atheist quality to the way in which Sāṃkhya drily investigates and then answers some of these questions. This has led some scholars to argue that the Sāṃkhya-Yoga approach sits somewhat apart from the metaphysics of the other early root texts, which each subscribe to the authority of the Vedas in explicit ways and which resolve existential divisions through *brahman*, a non-dual (and impersonal) principle that constitutes all of reality.[2] Indeed, so unusual was the dualism of Sāṃkhya-Yoga metaphysics that later commentators – primarily from Vedānta but also from Śaivism[3] – sought to resolve it in a non-dual synthesis that sublimated *prakṛti* and *puruṣa* into a higher unitary principle of *brahman*. But the root texts themselves, the *Sāṃkhyakārikā* and the *Yogasūtra*, do not easily lend themselves to this interpretation – as we will see in our discussion of theism, below.

In many senses, the *Yogasūtra* is working out the longstanding tension between action and non-action in early Indian philosophy (see also Chapter 7: Ethics). The importance of action is reflected not only in the theory of karmic retribution (the ethical consequences of action), but also in the older Vedic primacy of ritual action (as reflected in Patañjali's Vedic-inflected formula of *kriyā yoga*).[4] On the whole, however, the *Pātañjalayogaśāstra* reflects a world in which the gnostic soteriology of the *Upaniṣad*s has won out. In the tension between archaic Vedic action (ritual) and newer emphases on rational knowledge (philosophical contemplation), knowledge clearly wins the day as the means to become liberated. This does not mean that there is no place for action: materiality and consciousness are co-dependent. Likened respectively to 'the blind' and 'the lame' (SK 21), one cannot see and the other cannot act, and so both principles are co-fundamental to reality.

Perfect consciousness alone (*puruṣa*) cannot constitute reality, and its contentless (translucent) awareness is meaningless without the objective referent of materiality. Hence, even in the primacy of consciousness there is always the knower and the known, the seer and the seen (i.e. consciousness and materiality).

However, the explanation of how contact occurs between the knower and the known in this dualist metaphysics, while framed as a non-causal relation (and hence strictly dualist), is at times ambiguous. There are some puzzling statements that appear to undermine the notion of strict dualism – those that grapple with the concept of proximity as an alternative to causality for describing the relation between subject and object. For instance, at PYŚ 2.17–2.18 we are told that objects are like magnets for consciousness. Although this proximal relation is designed to sidestep causality, it implies that consciousness cannot help but be attracted or drawn to the magnetic objective world. We can resolve this somewhat, however, by recalling the notion that *puruṣa* has no agency (cannot act) and is, rather, a witness of the entire material world – like someone spectating action on a screen. Although consciousness is attracted to the spectacle of materiality, it does not (and indeed cannot) interact with the unfolding events it witnesses.

Realism or idealism?

What is implied in this metaphysical dualism is a possibility of both realist and idealist readings. If we refine our definition of realism from 'a world that is mind-independent' to 'a world that is consciousness-independent', then we could read the *prakṛti*/*puruṣa* division as indicating a realist metaphysics. Moreover, we find a clear refutation of idealism at YS 2.22 in which it is asserted that even though the objective world (*dṛśya*, i.e. the seen) comes to an end when liberation occurs, it does not stop existing in general for all minds, only for a particular individuated consciousness. For other minds, the world carries on.

Yet other statements contradict this. If, as we are told, *prakṛti* exists for the sake of consciousness (PYŚ 2.18),[5] then there is no such independence and, if anything, the opposite of realism is implied. This passage suggests an idealist worldview in which the existence of the material world is highly dependent on consciousness and which only manifests upon the illumination of consciousness (a macro-version of the question 'does an object exist if no subject is cognizing it?').[6] PYŚ 2.18 tells us that the seen (*dṛśya*), i.e. the objective world, has only one purpose: to be seen by *puruṣa*, both for the sake of experience (or enjoyment) and of liberation (*apavarga*). Both consciousness and materiality, then, have a single purpose: the tendency towards self-illuminated consciousness. PYŚ 2.18 underlines this point: existential bondage is the failure to fulfil the purpose of *puruṣa*, and freedom is the fulfilment of said purpose.

There is an important caveat, however, in the case of *prakṛti*. Only manifest *prakṛti* (also called *liṅga*, with a mark or distinguishing feature) can be said to exist for the sake of *puruṣa*. In its primordial or unmanifest state (*aliṅga*, 'without a mark'), *prakṛti* does not exist for the sake of *puruṣa* but simply resides in its own eternal nature self-sufficiently (PYŚ 2.19). This makes sense: that which has no mark or feature (*aliṅga*) cannot be witnessed as an object. There is an interesting instance here, then, in which primordial materiality (a kind of primordial 'soup') is beyond the metaphysical dualism of consciousness and matter and perhaps, in its own separation from the witnessing gaze of consciousness, is also 'free'. Moreover, the non-dual quality of *prakṛti* is further highlighted; the primordial materiality (*aliṅga*) is neither being (*sat*) nor non-being (*asat*), perhaps harking back to the 'Creation Hymn' ('Nāsadīya') of the *Ṛg Veda* (quoted above).

Funes-Maderey (2017) argues for a reading of this dualist metaphysics as indicating 'not totally independent of each other' (2017: 43), if the very existence of *prakṛti* is understood as being based on a fundamental misperception: 'in this sense, the whole manifestation of the objective world (including the mind) is dependent on the "miscognition" of the conscious principle' (Funes-Maderey 2017: 43). However, the issue with this argument is that *puruṣa* as a principle of pure consciousness cannot be subject to a fault such as 'miscognition', and hence the fault is always in the (material) mind and not in consciousness. For Funes-Maderey, Patañjali is not 'completely anti-realis[t]' (Funes-Maderey 2017: 43), and we can agree that neither is he completely realist. In likening the traces of idealism in Patañjali's thought to that of Kant, Funes-Maderey concludes that although both philosophers strive 'to prove the reality of an objective world independent of the mind', they both achieve this by 'conceiving [of] time in an anti-realist way, that is, not independent of our modes of cognizing it' (Funes-Maderey 2017: 42).

The metaphysics of the *Yogasūtra* can never quite escape the tinge of idealism: if materiality exists for the sake of consciousness, and manifests only when the light of consciousness is proximate, then the material world comes into manifest expression when illuminated by consciousness and returns to the unmanifest state when the light of consciousness is absent. This cycle is often understood within a macro understanding of time, but it also explains how objects appear in consciousness in micro-time: in moments or instants. This Sāṃkhya-Yoga understanding is distinct from the Buddhist notion of objects appearing temporarily in awareness and then disappearing. Patañjali's view is more attuned to the Vedic notion of time cycles – objects cycle in and out of manifestation according to presence or absence of consciousness. What is not entirely clear in the *Yogasūtra*, however, is the answer to this question: if consciousness is eternal and unwavering, why is there the possibility for it to be illuminating or not illuminating matter? In other words, why is everything in materiality not illuminated *all the time and at once* by the light of consciousness? Although this would be overwhelming for subjectivity and entail a divine-like omniscience, its absence still has to be explained in an otherwise eternalist metaphysics. In short, proximity as spatial closeness only partly explains the dualist relation between consciousness and matter. One final question that remains unresolved in this non-causal dualism is: what comes first in the relation of *prakṛti* and *puruṣa*, proximity or illumination?

The gender of dualism

The second issue that problematizes any understanding of this dualist metaphysics as denoting a partnership of equals is the gendered identities attributed to *puruṣa* and *prakṛti*: of consciousness as masculine and materiality as feminine. Hence, social tropes of the role of women in the early common era are reflected in metaphors that characterize *prakṛti* in the *Yogasūtra*, and these sometimes connote an inferior status in comparison to *puruṣa*.

In an attempt to justify why a material reality would exist if consciousness is the prime facet of reality, the text sometimes resorts to the gender- or class-based idea that a being of inferior (social) rank exists for the pleasure of a more privileged subject. Hence in Sāṃkhya-Yoga, *prakṛti* is sometimes described as the dancing girl who performs for the master (SK 42) or as the property of the lord in a relation that is cast as feudal:

> by means of [*citta*] being seen by *puruṣa*, there exists a relationship of master and property.
>
> (PYŚ 1.4)[7]

Due to its sattvic nature, awareness or *buddhi* (= *citta*) is the part of the material self that most closely resembles consciousness, but it is still part of *prakṛti*. Ultimately, the true (i.e. enduring) nature of self is understood to be consciousness and not matter. Therefore, although the metaphysics upholds an equivalence between the two, the consequence of embracing this philosophy is that consciousness and subjectivity are privileged over materiality and objectivity. We can identify a distinction of sorts between the metaphysics of the text, in which the gendered principles of reality are equal, and an androcentric ontology in which the goal of the method is to realize one's true identity, which is gendered as masculine (consciousness). These gendered ideas can be traced back to the late Vedic canon in the dual image of two birds in the tree, one eating and one watching.[8] However, such gender values are not necessarily evident in the early Vedas in which, if anything, the gendered dualism is flipped. In that context, the primary Vedic goddess of note is Vāc, who presides over language, not only in its known expression to humans but in the totality of the abstract system of language itself. This idea of language – concomitant with concepts and words – is certainly closer to consciousness than to material reality and perhaps indicates that, in the transition from Vedic philosophical speculation to systematized philosophy (*darśana*), the understanding of an absolute feminine metaphysical principle transitioned from language and conceptuality to materiality. As a social trope, this would be concordant with what some scholars have argued about the diminishing status of women over the late first millennium BCE as *dharmaśāstra* literature was consolidated (Dhand 2008). In the ontology of the *Yogasūtra*, reflecting its social mores, it is not that materiality is less real than consciousness but, in the ultimate scheme of things, of lesser value.

There has been increasing gender-centric scholarship on the metaphysics of the *Yogasūtra*. Notably, Funes-Maderey, drawing on Merleau-Ponty's phenomenological conception of the 'flesh' and Irigaray's theory of 'the maternal-feminine', argues that there is a narcissistic quality to *puruṣa*'s perception of *prakṛti* as an object for his pleasure alone (Funes-Maderey 2019: 45). According to this feminist interpretation, *puruṣa* is recast as being like an unborn child that does not recognize its mother as the material condition that sustains it. Such an argument, of course, rejects Sāṃkhya as a system that is, ultimately, dualist and shares ground with a common philosophical reading today of the metaphysics of the *Yogasūtra* as non-dual (e.g. Whicher 2001). However, the lens I propose asks us to remain faithful to the metaphysics of the text in its expression as a dualist system, while recognizing that almost immediately in its historical reception (from Śaṅkara onwards, if we accept the *Vivaraṇa* as his eighth-century composition),[9] this was a difficult metaphysical position to reconcile with embodied practices that 'felt' the world in a non-dual way, combined with an irresistible and prevailing theistic trend in Hindu philosophy towards the non-dualism of *brahman-ātman*, *śiva-śakti* and *kṛṣṇa-rādha*.

Critique notwithstanding, Funes-Maderey does find hope in a single metaphor in the *Sāṃkhyakārikā* that expresses the possibility of a reciprocal ontology in which there is a recognition of the 'irreducible' body of 'the other' – a body of consciousness or a body of materiality (Funes-Maderey 2017: 48). We return to the analogy of *prakṛti* and *puruṣa* as resembling the journey of a 'blind' person leading a 'lame' person (SK 21) – symbolically, one subject can act and the other can see, but in order to progress they are mutually interdependent (one to provide physical support and one to see the way ahead). This casts the recognition of difference (of the other) from 'sexual difference' to 'ontological difference' as a productive condition of intersubjectivity. Yet, as always in Sāṃkhya, liberation is the perception of materiality as different from consciousness, and this perception causes materiality to cease existing for that particular *puruṣa*. Nonetheless, despite liberation resting on the effective dissolution of the material, the gendered metaphysical pairing of Sāṃkhya-Yoga offers the possibility of understanding *puruṣa* and *prakṛti* in a more equal subject-subject relation rather than a subject-object one.

Further positive readings of gendered metaphysics are found in Ashton's analysis (2020). Ashton's reframing of Sāṃkhya dualism using Goethe's theory of nature as 'organic' (spontaneous and non-systemic bursting forth) aims to rescue *prakṛti* from what he describes as a distorted commentarial portrayal as 'inert, unintelligent matter' (Ashton 2020: 35). Ashton's reading leads towards a more positive interpretation of *prakṛti* as the 'procreatrix' and the 'vital power of living nature' (2020: 26), a reading clearly supported by the images of 'maternal creativity' (2020: 20) found at SK 39–43. However, this interpretation is not without its limitations in that it may reinforce an essentialized Romantic conception of nature as feminine as per Goethe's lens – e.g. in the casting of *prakṛti* as 'the surging emissions of a playful procreatress that loves to hide "in broad daylight"' (2020: 5) or in the sexual and reproductive recasting of the relation between *puruṣa* and *mūlaprakṛti* as a 'fertile friction' (2020: 21), an 'outpouring or oppositional tension' (2020: 24) that creates manifest reality, 'a tensional polarity whose dialectical interplay begets the living phenomenon (*vyaktaprakṛti*)' (2020: 21). Although Ashton is rightly curious as to whether there are proto-tantric conceptions of nature in Sāṃkhya *prakṛti* that have been overlooked, he is less explicit about the way in which this reading of *mūla-* and *vyakta-prakṛti* (primordial and manifest materiality) reflects some of the later Kashmir Śaiva Pratyabhijñā understandings of the creative relation between *śiva* as consciousness and *śakti* as the creative power of consciousness – a theisized re-envisioning that is not necessarily evident in either the *Yogasūtra* or the *Sāṃkhyakārikā*.

The question of God

In the metaphysics of Sāṃkhya, the expression of reality is twofold: there is consciousness and there is materiality. No higher principle than these two exists – and there is no supreme or creator God. Indeed, a metaphysics in which reality is eternal and beginningless does not require a creator God to explain the engendering of the world. However, there is a concession to this idea – perhaps reflecting the growing popularity of theism in the early first millennium[10] – in the form of *īṣvara*. The term *īṣvara* meant 'lord' or 'master', but in the early first millennium was firmly assuming a theistic meaning of absolute or creator God. And yet the nature of a somewhat personified *īṣvara* in the *Yogasūtra* is described in only a handful of *sūtras* (YS 1.23–1.28) and with somewhat limited attributes that make the identification of *īṣvara* as a creator God highly ambivalent. *Īśvara* somehow elides the dualist metaphysics, being 'neither *pradhāna* [primordial materiality] nor *puruṣa*' (PYŚ 1.23). Rather, *īśvara* is a special kind of consciousness or *puruṣa* (YS 1.24), a *guru* or teacher even of the ancients (YS 1.26). It is omniscient (YS 1.25) and omnipresent (YS 1.26) – but notably not omnipotent. As *īśvara* is a special type of *puruṣa*, presumably the concept and state of consciousness is a prior principle.

> ***Īśvara* is that special consciousness (*puruṣa*) [which is] untouched by affliction, moral retribution (*karma*), moral maturation[11] and (mental) substratum.**
>
> **(PYŚ 1.24)**

Like *puruṣa*, *īṣvara* watches the world, but does not experience it nor intervene:

> It is as when the victory or defeat of warriors is attributed to the commander. But *īṣvara* is a particular *puruṣa*, who is untouched by experience of this kind.
>
> (PYŚ 1.24)

Nonetheless, despite this disengaged stance from the world, *īśvara* is not unmoved by the suffering of humanity. Imbued with the compassionate motive of assisting creatures who are trapped in endless *saṃsāra* (PYŚ 1.25), *īśvara* provides instruction in knowledge and *dharma*[12] by imparting the true doctrines to the first sages (*ṛṣis*) from whom the Vedas were distilled (PYŚ 1.25). Hence, the authoritative word of scripture is the gift of *īśvara* to humanity as a means to escape suffering, and knowledge of *īśvara* can only be accessed through scripture and no other means, not even perception or inference (PYŚ 1.24). (See also 'Chapter 4: Epistemology'.) This special consciousness, *īśvara*, is a model *puruṣa* that can transcend time and space. There is certainly a hint that when one knows oneself as *puruṣa*, one is close in nature to *īśvara*:

> Such obstacles as disease and so forth cease to exist because of contemplation on *īśvara*. There is also vision of one's own form. Just as *īśvara* is a *puruṣa* who is clear, isolated, and without [need of any] addition, so is one who discovers that he is a *puruṣa* who is conscious of (*pratisaṃvedin*) [his own] awareness (*buddhi*).
>
> (PYŚ 1.29)

When one masters this practice of contemplation on *īśvara*, the result is perfection in concentration (*samādhi*) (YS 2.45), accompanied by omniscient knowledge that transcends space and time, delivering insight into the true nature of reality, just as it is (*yathābhūtam*).

We can agree then that *īśvara* is an important principle in Pātañjala yoga and is central in distinguishing this school of thought from Sāṃkhya – which is resolutely non-theist. In later periods, some doxographers distinguished between the Yoga and Sāṃkhya schools, by referring to them both as forms of Sāṃkhya that were respectively *seśvara* (featuring *īśvara*) and *nirīśvara* (not including *īśvara*). Patañjali's description of *īśvara* also reflects his adherence to the ancient art of studying the Vedas, which includes *tapas* (austerity), *svadhyāya* (daily recitation) and *īśvarapraṇidhāna* (contemplation on *īśvara*) (collectively grouped in *pāda* 2 as the 'active method', *kriyā yoga*). However, the inclusion of *īśvara* can be interpreted as a concession to prevailing theism, a clumsy remnant or bricolage of worldviews, or even a later insertion (interpolation) to the text. Hence the account of *īśvara* is also threaded through with ambiguity. For example, in its description of *kriyā yoga*, PYŚ 2.12 instructs that contemplation on *īśvara* contains a range of alternatives to *īśvara*: the contemplation can be focused on *īśvara* or on one of three other figures – a personal deity, a great seer or a saint. The passage continues: whomsoever is the figure of focus, this type of contemplation will bring good *karma* to fructify immediately. This depiction casts *īśvara* as an ideal figure in virtue ethics, rather than God as such. And, arguably, regarding *īśvara*'s lack of omnipotence, even the yogin who has attained mastery, as a perfected one (*siddha*), has more god-like power than *īśvara* – since such a yogin can become minute in size, magnify oneself or indeed transcend any elemental form or barrier,[13] being endowed with self-mastery (*vaśitva*), sovereignty or lordship (*īśitṛtva*), omnipresence (going anywhere) and omnipotence (with thoughts immediately creating material reality) (PYŚ 3.45). Another instance in which the supreme power of the yogin is affirmed occurs at YS 3.49:

> Solely by discerning the difference between *sattva* and *puruṣa*, one has supreme control over all beings and [one has] omniscience.
>
> (YS 3.49)

We can perhaps settle on a definition of *īśvara* as one idealized expression of liberated consciousness, or a form/being of consciousness that is ambivalently theisized to suit prevailing trends. Above all, it is important to note that a lack of creative power in no way detracts from pure consciousness (*puruṣa*), which seeks no entanglement with materiality. Therefore the yogin who seeks omnipotence is admonished as being engaged in no less than a distraction to the ultimate goal of liberation (YS 3.37).

Causal relations between materiality and consciousness

On the whole, a casual relation between *puruṣa* and *prakṛti* is avoided. Causality within *prakṛti* is also, strictly speaking, avoided in favour of a theory of matter that unfolds or emerges from an already-existing primordial basis. However, getting to grips with the distinction between materiality and consciousness is a subtle process. Therefore, there is not a complete avoidance of the philosophical vocabulary of causation theory. The purpose of consciousness is to know materiality, and materiality is said to exist 'for the sake of *puruṣa*'. This mutual relation is glossed as pointing to not only a reason (*hetu*) (e.g. the reason or purpose for the existence of materiality is consciousness and vice versa), but also to a relation between instrumental cause (*nimitta*), or agent,[14] and material cause (*kāraṇa*) (PYŚ 2.19), or substance.

The *Yogasūtra* adheres to a Sāṃkhya doctrine known as 'the effect pre-exists in the cause' (*satkāryavāda*), which circumvents conventional theories of cause-and-effect (discussed below). However, PYŚ 2.23 tells us that primordial materiality (*pradhāna*) cannot be said to be stasis alone since it produces effects; neither can manifested materiality be considered activity alone since effects cannot be produced without a cause. The conclusion here is that there is some version of cause and effect in operation within *prakṛti* between its unmanifest (causal) and manifest (effected) states.

However, the same cannot be said of consciousness, nor of the relation between consciousness and materiality. For example, PYŚ 2.23 informs us that *adarśana* ('non-seeing' or 'wrong seeing') is the instrumental cause (*nimitta*) of the illusory conjunction (*saṃyoga*) of consciousness and materiality – a misperception that constitutes existential bondage (*saṃsāra*). Hence, bondage has an instrumental cause. However, the same cannot be true for freedom or liberation, *mokṣa*, which is always-already existent. And so the same passage explains that while freedom cannot be said to have a material cause (i.e. *prakṛti* as *kāraṇa*), it can be described as the absence (or cessation) of wrong knowledge (*adarśana*). Here, formal reasoning is used to sidestep causality as operational within consciousness or freedom. While such states cannot be said to be causal or to be caused, they can be framed as existing in the absence of certain other factors, such as nescience (since it is destroyed by correct knowledge). As far as *puruṣa* is concerned, when wrong knowledge is absent, freedom is present – this is different than claiming that freedom *is caused by* the presence of right knowledge. In short, bondage (as a feature of *prakṛti*) is said to be caused, but freedom (as the condition of isolated consciousness, *kaivalya*) cannot be said to be caused (PYŚ 2.23).

A further exposition on causality can be found at PYŚ 2.28, which discusses the nine material causes (*kāraṇa*s) (Wezler 1987), as expounded in and quoted from another (unnamed) *śāstra*. They are listed thus, with an example for each:

- origination (*utpatti*), the way that the mind gives rise to knowledge
- constancy (*sthiti*), the way that consciousness sustains the mind, like food sustains the body
- manifestation (*abhivyakti*), the way that seeing an object facilitates knowledge of that object
- modification (*vikāra*), the way that a new object appears in the mind, or the way that the addition of fire facilitates cooking
- ideation (*pratyaya*), inferential knowledge, such as seeing smoke brings about knowledge of fire
- realization (*āpti*), the way that practice of the yoga auxiliaries leads to attainment of discriminating discernment
- disjunction (*viyoga*), the way that the yoga auxiliaries produce disjunction from impurity
- difference (*anyatva*), the way that the goldsmith is different to gold

- supporting (*dhṛti*), the way that the body sustains the senses, the elements support the body, and all creatures and gods mutually support one another

From among these material causes, the yoga system is singled out as leading to two effects only: the disjunction from impurity (i.e. the reduction and elimination of the mental afflictions) and the acquisition of right knowledge (discriminating discernment) (PYŚ 2.28).

The finer points of these philosophical discussions of causation theory have not, perhaps, been grasped by all adepts who have encountered the *Yogasūtra* over history, since they are complex. But some simple promises are made about the results of the yoga method: in the discussion of *aṣṭāṅga yoga*, for example, we are given the straightforward assurance that the practice of the auxiliaries of yoga is the cause of disjunction (*viyogakāraṇam*) from impurity, just as *dharma* is the cause of happiness (and what is meant here is the happy state of discriminating discernment) (PYŚ 2.28). Interestingly, this causal relation is further qualified as producing a unique or singular effect; *aṣṭāṅga yoga* can lead to this state alone and cannot be the cause of any other outcome (PYŚ 2.28).

Being, time and causality

The overarching Sāṃkhya theory of time is cyclical, and time operates only in relation to materiality. *Puruṣa*, as unchanging pure consciousness, is not subject to time or space. Time, then, occurs in the realm of materiality (*prakṛti*), facilitating processes of emanation and dissolution (see Figure 1).[15] Furthermore, time does not have a beginning point, being eternal and endless. However, within this overarching frame of Pātañjala eternalism, there exist many nuanced and complex discussions of time.

Central to the Sāṃkhya theory of causality is the argument that 'the effect pre-exists in the cause' (*satkāryavāda*). This doctrine holds that the effect pre-exists in the cause in a potential state, and that change is then merely a transformation (*pariṇāma*) of what was already there. The text states:

> it is established that there is an immediate causal sequence, inasmuch as the condition of what is caused and its cause are not different even though separated.
>
> (PYŚ 4.9; trs. Larson 2018: 867)

Hence, cause and effect cannot be said to be distinct in condition or essence. As Chakrabarti explains:

> a clay pot is potentially in the lump of clay out of which it is fashioned, a statue is potentially in the rock out of which it is carved, oil is potentially in the oil seed, and so on.
>
> (Chakrabarti 1999: 181)

This allows for an explanation of the apparent continuity of events through time while simultaneously retaining the theory of materiality itself as permanently existing. This fact of change over time is strictly qualified, however, since even with formal changes in entities and their properties (*dharmas*),[16] the underlying individuated substance itself (*dharmin*) remains unaltered, and so the transformation in clay from powder to lump to cup to fragment[17] are changes that take place in time (sequence, *krama*) rather than in substance (PYŚ 3.15).

Since materiality (*prakṛti*) has an unmanifest ground that is timeless, even when objects manifest in the material realm or in our senses, they are also always part of a prior unchanging 'soup' of time. In the cycles of emanation and dissolution, temporal travelling and unfolding is not so much linear as like a loop. Much like *puruṣa*'s unchanging state of no-content, materiality too has a primordial state of changelessness, which is the ground of time.

Time is understood to be constituted of past, present and future, which are distinct phases of temporality. Indeed, PYŚ 3.13 engages in a highly technical discussion of this relation through a scathing critique of the Buddhist Sarvāstivāda Abhidharma school which maintains that past/present/future are one, known as the 'three time periods' doctrine or 'tri-temporality'. Patañjali rejects this simultaneity doctrine baldly: 'However, there can be no simultaneous manifestation of living entities because of the interrelation of place, time, form and cause' (PYŚ 3.14). This specific example explains that in reincarnation theory a self cannot instantiate in several bodies at once since reincarnation happens in a sequence of multiple lives over time, disproving the claim that past/present/future are one. But the statement is also part of a wider discussion on how entities (*dharmas*) transform over time and how to reconcile this fact with an overarching ontology of permanence. Interestingly, the past is singled out as particularly redundant in any theory of change as 'sequential'. It is observed that such transformation (of the clay into powder, jar, fragment and so on) is only meaningful in the sequential transition from present to future. No such changes can be implemented retrospectively into the past (PYŚ 3.15), even if changes from past states can, of course, be observed from a present vantage point.

When assessing Patañjali's doctrine of *satkāryavāda*, it is important to remember that it is first and foremost a core tenet of the Sāṃkhya school. Ashton's discussion of the question of cause and effect in the *Sāṃkhyakārikā* is therefore instructive (Ashton 2020). Ashton is concerned with how the later Śaiva Pratyabhijñā school promotes a faulty interpretation of Sāṃkhya dualism. He therefore rejects the common interpretation of *satkāryavāda* (the effect pre-existing in the cause) as indicating the utter singularity/uniformity of *prakṛti*, by appealing for a starker ontological distinction between primordial or root materiality (*mūlaprakṛti*) and manifest materiality (*vyaktaprakṛti*). For Ashton, manifest materiality is an effect of the former in the sense that it is its own self-generating cause and does not require the proximity of *puruṣa* to instigate change. Ashton's interpretation of *satkāryavāda* as a doctrine of 'intensification of living nature' (2020: 27) rather than emanation rejects 'scientific models of causality (material, efficient, final)' (2020: 23 fn70) in favour of Goethean understandings of the process such as: an '*Urphänomenon* that metamorphizes' (23), an 'organized becoming' (23), a 'spontaneous, organic intensification' (22). In sticking closely to the context of the *Pātañjalayogaśastra*, however, I focus on an alternative explanation next.

Contiguity (not continuity); proximity (not causality)

Patañjali tends to justify material continuity through notions of force and contiguity rather than causal process (PYŚ 4.10). As Maas has discussed (2020), at certain points in the text, Patañjali delicately reworks various Buddhist theories of time[18] to make them fit into a Sāṃkhya metaphysics. The theory he reworks is by the Sarvāstivāda Buddhists, the claim that the progression of time is an illusion and that the past, present and future all exist in the present moment. At PYŚ 3.13, Maas argues, Patañjali combined the Sarvāstivāda Abhidharma theories in a novel way to transpose them from a Buddhist position (all conditioned factors are subject to transitoriness) to a Sāṃkhya-Yoga position (the transformation of substance has a permanent substratum even through time). Positing direct engagement with Buddhist philosophers, Maas shows that *Yogasūtra* 3.13 rewords a passage from Vasubandhu's *Abhidharmakośabhāṣya*, reworks Dharmatrāta's theory of the momentariness of conditioned factors in the *Vibhāṣā* and modifies the theories of Ghoṣaka, Vasumitra and Buddhadeva. In Maas's conclusion, Patañjali's reformulation was used as a polemic device in order to reorient a Sarvāstivāda ontology towards Sāṃkhya (Maas 2020).

Another instance of interaction with Buddhist theories of causality is in Patañjali's theory of the mind as having a permanent ontological substratum that transfers between multiple incarnations. Patañjali posits an interesting notion of time to account for the way in which seeds of self transmigrate from one moment of existence to another, including after the point of physical death. Rather than a linear movement through time and space (i.e. travelling from one point in time and one body to another), the seeds are said to have contiguous properties, whereby the seeds themselves do not travel, but have an inherent capacity or propensity that can be transferred (re)productively as if through a sequence of moments, although in fact through a proximal and contiguous endowment of capacity (O'Brien-Kop 2018). Hence change is happening in materiality all at once in a kind of spatial transference of properties, rather than a temporal transference. This leads us back to *satkāryavāda* as a basic idea that 'everything is everything' all at once but with continuous modification.

A further example of contiguity is in the framing of the relation between *prakṛti* and *puruṣa* as a proximal relation and not a causal relation. Patañjali posits a theory of causality, but only in relation to materiality and not to consciousness. Subtle causality in *prakrti* (emanation and dissolution of *tattvas*, or the reason for materiality 'with a mark', *liṅga*) can be traced all the way back to the state of primordial unmanifestness (*pradhāna* = *aliṅga* or 'without a mark'): 'There is not a further [prior] subtle object beyond the *aliṅga*' (PYŚ 1.45). When an interlocutor raises the objection that surely *puruṣa* is a subtle cause in some way, this notion is rejected:

> this does not apply to *puruṣa*, since *puruṣa* is not the consequential cause of manifest materiality (*liṅga*) but is the reason (*hetu*). Therefore the subtlety of unmanifest materiality (*pradhāna*) is explained as unsurpassed.
>
> (PYŚ 1.45)

Primordial materiality (*pradhāna* or *mūlaprakṛti*) is unsurpassed, meaning that is has no cause. *Puruṣa* is entirely disentangled from the material world of cause and effect and yet, by its very proximity and its nature as light (luminosity) (discussed in 'Chapter 8: Aesthetics'), its co-presence is a non-causal condition, a motivation perhaps, for *prakṛti* to evolve.[19]

Due to the lack of involvement of consciousness with the world, liberation itself is a paradoxical concept in that it is outside time. In this key sense, *puruṣa* is always already liberated and hence undergoes no transformation. The ending of illusion or the experience of escape resides only in awareness or *buddhi* and when *buddhi* dissolves, *puruṣa* remains unchanging (PYŚ 2.15). Furthermore, we are told that the essence (*svarūpa*) of *puruṣa* is not something to be acquired since this would subject it to causality (*hetuvāda*) (PYŚ 2.15). Again, the strict dualist metaphysics prevails, and so even self-realization is not a process that is caused, since consciousness is always inherently true and stable, simply waiting to be glimpsed self-consciously. Interestingly, even ethical causality is mapped according to the same principles as material causality. In the way that the gross aspects of materiality produce the subtle in ever-evolving flows, so does the experience of suffering produce a stock of subtle karmic imprints of affective suffering in a process that is called 'a beginningless stream' (PYŚ 2.15).

Universals and particulars

Like the other philosophical schools of the period, Pātañjala yoga accounts for reality, what it consists of and how we can perceive its constituent parts. In these discussions of ontology, we see the deep interconnections with other systems of thought, such as Vaiśeṣika, a school dedicated to describing the smallest particles of reality that exist. Such arguments about how the various dimensions of reality can be quantified and classified, using combinations of 'universal' qualities and 'particular' qualities, were quite simply part of the philosophical pursuit. Additionally, however, in a system that is geared towards correct knowledge of materiality (and its difference from consciousness), it was essential for Patañjali to propose a theory of how to scrutinize and correctly perceive objects and substances, since this method of rational reflection (or discriminating discernment) is the very basis of the meditative method.

The *Yogasūtra* explains that matter is not just what we can see. As well as physical, there are essential or subtle aspects to materiality, which are linked to the ontological notions of universals and particulars. For example, water has a universal form of liquidity (which is visible), but the particular properties of any one body of water may vary in temperature, salinity, etc. (which are not necessarily visible). Furthermore, an additional implication of the doctrine that the effect pre-exists in the cause (*satkāryavāda*), sometimes glossed as 'everything is everything,'[20] means that class distinctions between objects are provisional or conventional. Hence, the apparent fact of genus-species (*jāti*) divisions is superseded by a doctrine that claims that, ultimately, there is just one material phenomenon, *prakṛti*.[21] Since a thing is a combination of universals and particulars (a 'jug' that is 'blue/old/large/empty/chipped, etc.'), there is no separate 'whole' distinct from its 'parts', in that the whole is bound up in the constellation (or conglomeration) of the particulars. Therefore, the whole cannot be categorized separately or meaningfully into genus-species boxes (that 'blue jug' above may have little in common with a jug that is 'made of jade/pristine/ornamental/engraved/without handles, etc.').

Yoga ontology takes its lead not only from Sāṃkhya but also from other schools such as Vaiśeiṣika. Among the key material categories in Patañjali's ontology, is *dravya*, or substance. *Dravya* is an important term in Pātañjala philosophy and can mean both 'thing' in general but also 'ontologically real substance', and 'substrate substance'. One important discussion of *dravya* takes place at PYŚ 3.13. *Dravya* indicates material substance, but it can take individuated forms called the *dharmin* (discussed below). One such individuated substance is gold and it is an example that is used to illustrate the theory of material change: the temporal modalities (past, present and future) produce different conditions or states (*avasthā*) of gold, but not a different substance. In short, gold is still gold across time whether it is old or new, a bracelet or a vessel, a minute amount or a vast quantity. An object, then, is always a modification of an original substance in the way that a gold bracelet is shaped from a basis of gold, and is not substantially different to that gold.

Of course, there are composite substances, which require a slightly different argument. Hence, a tree or a cow is a 'substance' in which the specific differences (of sap/bark/root, etc. or of flesh/hide/hair, etc.) are no longer relevant to categorization. Substantially, we recognize a tree or a cow as a single entity. This is quite different from plural collections of entities, such as 'a forest' (made up of trees) or 'a herd' (made up of cows) (PYŚ 3.44). Only the first category (the 'cow', the 'tree') expresses the notion of substance (*dravya*), which has an essence (*svarūpa*) that is made up of the universal and particular (PYŚ 3.44). Although classification can be made on the basis of difference or identity, a substance – and this is stated as Patañjali's definitive view – is a entity in which the specific parts cannot be meaningfully separated while retaining the whole (PYŚ 3.44).[22]

Hence, the *Pātañjalayogaśāstra* describes material substance, *dravya*, as having a nature that is both universal and particular, both general and specific (*sāmānyaviśeṣātmaka*).

Linking universals-particulars to cause-effect

This ontology is underpinned by the broader understanding of materiality. Although, as mentioned above, consciousness is plural in essence, *prakṛti* is singular in essence – and so the divisions of the 23 constituents (*tattvas*) are only apparent in their distinction. The *tattvas* are not ontologically separate and are emanations from a single *dravya* (i.e. *prakṛti* itself). Mohanty relates the universal-particular to cause-effect theory: *prakṛti* as a universal is the ultimate cause, while the effects are the particulars (*tattvas*) in material reality (Mohanty 2000: 58). However, as discussed below, this raises some problems because it positions *prakṛti* as an ultimate cause, which is difficult to reconcile with a strict interpretation of eternalism and permanence (time and materiality without beginning or end). Beyond the physical, *dravya* also has a subtle aspect which we might call the intangible (sound, touch, form/colour, taste and smell), said to exist in atomic form (*aṇu*) and which also has an inherent essence (*svarūpa*) and particularity (*viśeṣa*) (PYŚ 3.44). Furthermore, substances have an internal relation between the three qualities of balance, inertia and dynamism (*sattva, tamas, rajas*), which produces a kind of internal causality in the substance. Substances can be said to produce effects, but only those that are essentially seeded by their own nature, *svarūpa*. Hence a mango tree can only be produced from a mango seed, and not an apple seed – again, drawing on the Sāṃkhya doctrine of the effect pre-existing in the cause (*satkāryavāda*). The existence of these substances (*dravya*) in the world is said to have a purpose of objectivity – i.e. to manifest as objects in the world.

Rational reflection on the nature of materiality

Physical or gross materiality (*sthūla*) is categorized as having the properties of inherent essence (*svasāmānya*), subtle form (*sūkṣma*), relations (*anvaya*) and purpose or objectivity (*artha*) (PYŚ 3.44). For physical/gross substances that belong to the same class (such as the class of 'earth' substances or 'water' substances), the differences between them are only a reflection of properties (*dharma*)[23] and not of the underlying substrate (*dharmin*) itself, e.g. the substrate of 'earth'.[24] It is only by contemplating this assertion that one can arrive at a true perception of the nature of materiality, as singular and undivided. An example might be as follows: by contemplating a property or *dharma* such as liquidity, one gains understanding of the individuated substance (*dharmin*) of water which, in turn, will lead one to perceive the underlying material substrate (*prakṛti*) of the world – and perhaps even glimpse the primordial matter (*mūlaprakṛti*) that gives rise to it. Why is this important? Because understanding pure consciousness is a challenge for an embodied being – it is much easier to start with the world around us and to scrutinize its depths. By this rational process, we are led to perceive the material domain for what it is – and for what it is not, i.e. consciousness.

The *Pātañjalayogaśāstra* proposes that rational reflection on the five aspects of substance (physical, essential, subtle, relational, purposive) yields a control over the manifest objective world:

> Because of this control, the active functioning of various elements runs[25] parallel to the intention of the yogin, like cows follow their own calves.
>
> (PYŚ 3.44; trs. Larson 2018: 783)[26]

This statement can be read as idealist, i.e. that through a true understanding of the nature of material reality, materiality itself is entrained to behave and appear according to the intention of the yogin. Interestingly, this larger ontological argument is employed again in the case of the material self. Like the objective world, the material self can be truly known and controlled, if subjected[27] to rational reflection on its fivefold nature (cognition, inherent essence, egoity, relations and objective purpose). Such reflection follows a pattern of advanced regression, moving from the outer world to the inner self, which brings an understanding of the underlying substances (*dravya*) of one's own being, e.g. mind (=material). The essence (*svarūpa*) of self also holds collocations that are indivisible substances, such as a sense capacity. What is important in rational reflection on the material world or on the self is that the object is approached by the five techniques in sequence. This progressive analysis leads one to ever more subtle levels of understanding. To place these two processes next to each other:

External/objective:
Gross matter > inherent essence > subtlety > relations (causal) > objective purpose (YS 3.44)

Internal/subjective:
Cognition > inherent essence > egoity > coherence (causal) > objective purpose (YS 3.47)

In both cases, the outcome of rational reflection is control of the material domain. We are led back to the notion that the purpose of materiality is for the sake of *puruṣa*, i.e. to be witnessed by consciousness and seen for what it truly is.

Substance and change

As we have ascertained, there is often a delicate balance in Pātañjala ontology in how to account for change within a worldview that is based on eternalism. For Patañjali, the material world is composed of a single substrate substance or *dravya* (i.e. *prakṛti*), but in individuated expression the substance is a *dharmin* (PYŚ 3.13). However, the *dharmin*[28] (let's say gold) is subject to change in three ways: in its characteristic or property (*dharma*), in its temporal mode (*lakṣana*) and in its overall state or condition (*avasthā*).[29] Hence a shiny, new, fashionable bracelet may, over time, become dull, old and a relic – but the fact of its 'goldness' never changes. Patañjali's commentary includes standard objections from a philosophical opponent (*pūrvapakṣin*), who identifies an apparent contradiction in Patañjali's argument: that there is a permanent and eternal substratum to reality, but also that change can and does happen in the world.

> Another sets forth (an objection). The basic substance (*dharmin*)[30] cannot be separated from its attributes or characteristics (*dharma*-s), since its prior condition (*pūrva-tattva*) is not surpassed [that is, does not change]. If it [the substance] could be the same, including or following upon the distinctions of the conditions of prior and subsequent, it would then entail being eternal or everlasting (which is contradictory).
>
> (PYŚ 3.13; trs. Larson 2018: 633)

In sum, the opponent asks this question: how can reality be permanent *and* changing at the same time? Patañjali's answer is that such an objection is wrongly founded, since 'the (absolute) uniformity of the substance (*dharmin*) has not been asserted' (PYŚ 3.1.3; trs. Larson 2018: 633). Neither has it been asserted that the manifest world is permanently static, rather that it is permanently existing. For Patañjali, manifested material reality is subject to change and decay. It is only primordial materiality (in potentiate) that remains unchanging forever. Patañjali employs several different names for this primordial matter or energy:

- *pradhāna* or 'primordial'
- *mūlaprakṛti*, 'base/root materiality'
- *aliṅga* or 'unmarked' (*aliṅga* PYŚ 2.19), i.e. materiality with no distinct features
- *avyakta* or the 'unmanifest' (PYŚ 2.18)

Additionally, even when manifest, materiality is dissolved back into the primordial soup, there is not 'nothing', since the world still exists. In periods or cycles of devolved material reality, there is still a subtle framework of material reality (time and space); it is simply that no individuated material substance (*dharmin*) exists. A further point is that the triad of characteristic-temporality-state cannot really be disentangled. A clay pot (made from an underlying substance of clay) changes in characteristic, temporal feature and state as it moves from 'new pot' to 'old pot' to 'disintegrated pot'. Yet these three levels of change are not separate, but very much part of a continuum. That is to say, any changes to characteristic-temporality-state are restricted by the essential nature of the *dharmin*, in this case clay – i.e. because it is made of clay, the pot cannot grow wings, turn neon yellow and fly into the sky as it ages. Hence, the three changes

> do not go beyond the essential nature of the substance (*dharmin*), which means that there is only a single type of change that encompasses all these particular modalities.
>
> (PYŚ 3.1.3; trs. Larson 2018: 636)

The changes to a clay pot cannot be just any changes, but those that are restricted by the nature of clay itself; they are entailed (like the mango seed entails a mango tree and not an apple tree). The commentary to sutra 3.13 sums up the overall arguments on change concisely:

> Change (*pariṇāma*) is the arising of empirical differentiations out of the cessation (or transformations or mutations) of earlier empirical differentiations of an abiding substance (*dravya*).
>
> (PYŚ 3.1.3; trs. Larson 2018: 636)

Without the 'abiding substance', change itself could not be observed or measured. Hence it is not the *dharmin* (individuated substance such as clay or gold) that is subject to change but the properties of the entity (the clay pot or the gold bracelet). And the distinction between the two is central to this yogic ontology:

> A *dharma* (entity with properties) is merely the capacity of the *dharmin* (individuated substance), made distinct as appropriate. *Dharma* is [this] capacity alone.
>
> (PYŚ 3.14)

In this relation, it is the *dharmin* which is prior to the *dharma* ontologically (PYŚ 3.13), and within this argument we also see the doctrine of *satkāryavāda* expressed. Although the present effects can be perceived directly, the substance must be inferred. It is not always evident as to what a painted pot is made from – underneath the paint it might be made from clay, but it might be made from gold. Again, this ontology sits within the broader metaphysics of the text. All of these arguments about substrate substance (*dravya*) and individuated substance (*dharmin*) can be related to the broader point that there is only one substrate of the material world, *prakṛti*. Although apparently plural in form and subject to change, objects are merely transformations of a single ontological principle (*prakṛti*). This fundamental understanding of reality is one half of the endeavour, but it supports one in correctly perceiving the rest of reality – and to see that consciousness is not part of the material world and is as plural as *prakrti* is singular. These rational reflections are valuable as theoretical exercises, but are also the integral method of Patañjali's yoga philosophy – it is only by understanding reality truthfully that we can attain existential freedom.

Discussion questions

1. The *Yogasūtra* argues that the mind is a material phenomenon. How does this sit with contemporary neuroscience which argues that the mind is an effect of the brain?
2. Is a dualist metaphysics compatible with embodied experience of the world?
3. To what degree are gendered notions pertaining to consciousness and matter/nature reflected in your society today?
4. In your worldview, what does reality consist of and how does change occur? Is there more continuity or more change in the world?

Further reading

Ashton, G. (2020) 'The Puzzle of Playful Matters in Non-Dual Śaivism and Sāṃkhya: Reviving *Prakṛti* in the *Sāṃkhya Kārikā* through Goethean Organics' in *Religions* 115: 221. 1–38.

Burley, M. (2007) *Classical Sāṃkhya and Yoga: An Indian Metaphysics of Experience*. London and New York: Routledge.

Chakravarti, P. (1975) *Origin and Development of the Sāṃkhya System of Thought*. Delhi: Oriental Books Reprint Corp.

Harimoto, K. (2014) *God, Reason, and Yoga: A Critical Edition and Translation of the Commentary Ascribed to Śaṅkara on Pātañjalayogaśāstra*. Hamburg: University of Hamburg.

Howard, V. (2019) 'Gender Conceptions in Indian Thought: Identity, Hybridity, Fluidity, Androgyny and Transcendence' in Howard, V. (ed.) *The Bloomsbury Research Handbook of Indian Philosophy and Gender*. London and New York: Bloomsbury Academic.

Funes-Maderey, A. (2019) 'The Unbearability of the Male Gaze. An Exposition of Sāṃkhyan Philosophy of Embodiment through "Feminine" Phenomenological Eyes' in Howard, V. (ed.) *Indian Philosophy and Gender*. New York and London: Bloomsbury Publishing.

Khandelwal, M. (2010). *Women in Ochre Robes: Gendered Hindu Renunciation*. Albany: SUNY.

Larson, G. (1969) *Classical Sāṃkhya: An Interpretation of Its History and Meaning*. Delhi: Motilal Banarsidass Publishers Private Limited.

Motegi, S. (2013) 'The Early History of Sāṃkhya Thought' in Franco, E. (ed.) *Historiography and Periodization of Indian Philosophy*. Vienna: De Nobili Research Library.

Sinha, B. (1983) *Time and Temporality in Sāṃkhya-Yoga and Abhidharma Buddhism*. New Delhi: Munshiram Manoharlal Publishers.

3

Ontology: Self and being

Chapter outline

Ontology is a branch of philosophy situated within metaphysics. It is the study of being and its nature and often asks questions such as: Who am I? What is my nature? What are the constituents of reality? In the previous chapter, we began to examine ontology in relation to the constitution of the objective world, and how it is affected by time and change. In this chapter, we turn to subjectivity and the key ontological questions on the constitution of the self and how to know the self.

What is the self?

For most schools of thought in Early Indian Philosophy, the theoretical and practical quest is to know the self in order that one may experience existential freedom. The *Pātañjalayogaśāstra* is no exception to this goal.

The ideal subject of Patañjali's text is an ascetic practitioner called a *yogin*, meaning that the type of ascetic contemplation that he practices (and it was normatively a 'he' historically) was known as 'yoga'. As discussed in 'Chapter 1: Introduction', the primary meaning of 'yoga' in early Hindu and Buddhist treatises was various forms of meditation, contemplation or rational reflection. The goal of philosophical meditation is to enter states of cognitive clarity in which one can accurately perceive reality as it truly is – including the self. Indeed, the very existential problem that Indian philosophy strives to resolve is that of nescience (*avidyā*), the erroneous perception of the self and one's environment, which produces suffering. Depending on the school of thought, suffering was defined doctrinally in different ways. Most schools in the Hindu tradition, for example, posited the self to be unchanging and eternal, framed as a macro-self (such as *brahman*) with transcendent properties and/or as an individual self in a material and temporal instantiation (such as *ātman*).

The *Pātañjalayogaśāstra* adheres to these conceptions, although it uses its own technical vocabulary to describe the self. In fact, the more abstract term *ātman* (self) is employed relatively infrequently. One example is within a quotation cited at PYŚ 1.36:

> 'He who cognizes that the self (*ātman*) is [merely] the size of an atom is thus truly conscious of 'I am' (*asmitā*)'.
>
> (PYŚ 1.36)

Here, the term *asmitā* is used to positively elucidate the subjective specificity of self as 'I am' (see also YS 1.17), i.e. *puruṣa*, which is said to be 'luminous' (PYŚ 1.36). Moreover:

> Then the mind that has arrived at 'I am' (*asmitā*) manifests only 'I am' that is eternally peaceful, like a motionless great ocean.
>
> (PYŚ 1.36)

However, there is also a negative meaning to *asmitā*, when there is an erroneous conception of self, such as a cognitive mix-up between consciousness and awareness, i.e. the mind:

> When the power of the seer, *puruṣa*, and the power of seeing, *buddhi*, are both reduced to one form, this affliction is called *asmitā*.
>
> (PYŚ 2.6)

In no way should the highest function of mind, intelligent awareness or *buddhi*, be misunderstood as the self (*ātman*), as underlined by this embedded quotation from the Sāṃkhya thinker Pañcaśikha:

> Thus it is said: 'He who does not see (*apaśyan*) that the *puruṣa* is beyond the *buddhi* – distinct in form, nature, and knowledge, etc – would make the *buddhi* into the *ātma* by means of delusion'.
>
> (PYŚ 2.6)[1]

Clearly *puruṣa* and *ātman* are one and the same – and sometimes *asmitā* is even a synonym for consciousness. But the mind-complex (*citta*) and intelligent awareness (*buddhi*) are distinct from consciousness, since they belong to the material domain.

Another key term in the analysis of self is the false apprehension of the self as 'egoity' or *ahaṃkāra*, which takes placed in the material complex of the mind (see also 'Chapter 4: Epistemology'). When one misunderstands the self as the ego, this is a false apprehension of *asmitā* ('I am'). Nonetheless *asmitā* as 'egoity' has an important function doctrinally, since it also provides an effective counterpart to the Buddhist notion of *anātman* (non-self), i.e. that there is no stable 'I' that is real. However, as we have seen, the concept of *ātman* is only sketched in the *Pātañjalayogaśāstra*, in comparison to other Brahmanical texts of the period.

To summarize so far: Drawing on the metaphysics of the Sāṃkhya school of thought, the *Pātañjalayogaśāstra* argues for an irreconcilable dualism between consciousness on the one hand and mind and body on the other. Essential to this text's ontology is the clear location of the mind in the realm of materiality, where the body also resides. Consciousness, in contrast, exists in a co-fundamental but radically separate sphere of reality.

The many techniques of Pātañjala yoga are all geared to a simple outcome: the ability of consciousness to recognize itself in essence. In line with the Sāṃkhya metaphysics of the text, the essential self is true (consciousness, *puruṣa*) and the non-essential self is false (materially and temporally bound, *prakṛti*). Self-consciousness therefore entails a disengagement from the false self, both epistemologically and ontologically.

Yet, the nature of the true self as consciousness or the focus on mental techniques do not mean that the body is excluded from the philosophical enquiry of yoga. The body is an ancillary aspect of identity and is independent of the true self; when the body perishes, the consciousness endures without a flicker of response, simply becoming associated with another corporeal vehicle at some point (unless the state of freedom has been attained, in which case those cycles of association end). This understanding of consciousness is, in itself, hard to grasp, not just for the subject/yogin of the text but for us, the contemporary readers. This is because the ontology of the text is informed by a radical dualism that is different from a European Cartesian dualism of mind-body. Rather, Patanjali's opposition is between consciousness and a unitary mind-body complex. Nonetheless, in the acquisition of true perception, one has to start somewhere, and so the main entry point to this philosophical practice is the body. In the pairing of practice and dispassion laid out in the first *pāda* (PYŚ 1.12), it is practice that leads to dispassion:

> What are the means for the restriction of [mental] fluctuations? **They are ceased by practice and dispassion**.
>
> (PYŚ 1.12)[2]

Dispassion develops incrementally as an increasingly diminished corporeal engagement with the material world (a withdrawal) and, ultimately, as the dispassionate (conscious) view of one's material self.

On the whole, however, the body does not figure centrally in the *Pātañjalayogaśāstra*'s definition of self.[3] This may seem like a contestable point, but the role of the body in the text has been overplayed by at least two historical frames: the first is Indian scholastic commentary and the second is modern anachronistic readings of fourth-century Pātañjala yoga as a body-oriented practice. Both of these frames emphasize the 'eightfold method' (discussed below), the section of the text in which the body is most visibly foregrounded. Yet what Patanjali's treatise primarily outlines is a philosophy of mind centred on mundane and transcendent complexes of self that exist through cognition, juxtaposing the mind (*citta*) with consciousness (*puruṣa*). The text therefore delineates various techniques to bring about the state of knowledge that is understood as existential freedom and as a disembodied mode of being.

The treatise opens with the maxim 'Yoga is the cessation of the fluctuations of the mind' (*yogaś cittavṛttinirodhaḥ*) (YS 1.2), identifying the mind (*citta*) as the problem (its activity must be stopped) and not the body (which has a more subsidiary role to play). As mentioned, the text proffers practice (*abhyāsa*) and dispassion (*vairāgya*) as the two means to achieve mental cessation (YS 1.12). As discussed in 'Chapter 1: Introduction', Pātañjala yoga delineates not just one but several pathways of practice, knitted together. None of these schemes focuses on the body – it is only ever a gateway or preliminary point of attention.

The goal of Pātañjala yoga is to reside in a state of isolated consciousness, free of the body and mind, and one of the key means to reach the ideal state is discriminating discernment (*vivekakhyāti*), specifically to distinguish the true self from the false self. Erroneous cognition produces

> the perception of self in non-self – through external instruments, be they animate or inanimate, or in the body, which is the basis of enjoyment, or in the mind, which is an object for consciousness (*puruṣa*) – these are all perception of self in non-self.
>
> (PYŚ 2.5)

Discriminating discernment, on the other hand, refers to the ability to know the difference between the principles of consciousness and materiality, and ultimately to disembody that very difference: when one realizes that one's true nature is consciousness (*puruṣa*), rather than the material mind or body, then one attains philosophical and spiritual liberation. In this radically dualist ontology, then, true knowledge is always about the disembodiment of the self.

The nature of consciousness

If liberated consciousness is not in some way attached to a material subjectivity (a body), then how are we to understand such a disembodied reality? What does this mean for subjectivity? These are complex questions that scholars continue to pore over. The text does not prescribe that the body should perish, i.e. die for liberation to occur; but one's adoption of the witnessing state of consciousness is permanent (i.e. there is no reverting to nescience). Therefore, one's consciousness remains associated with a corporeal existence (as long as it continues), but is supremely detached from it. This is a radical, permanent ontological transformation and shift from awareness (*buddhi*) to consciousness (*puruṣa*), which undergoes no future mutation. Awareness, because it is associated with the mind and materiality, is restricted or limited in knowledge and perspective, even in its purest state. Consciousness, on the other hand, has no such restriction and therefore facilitates self-consciousness.

How are contemporary audiences to relate to such an ideal? In everyday terms, Patañjali's freedom indicates a life that is permanently informed by a watchful consciousness that understands its own perfect detachment from the ups and downs of life's events, emotions and vagaries – and even from death itself. This is a significant variation of the detachment-in-action proposed by another key philosophical text of the period, the *Bhagavad Gītā*, which also draws on Sāṃkhya metaphysics.[4] But unlike the *Bhagavad Gītā*'s theistic presentation of a supreme consciousness, the *Yogasūtra* asserts that consciousness has no ultimate or absolute locus. It is plural and countless in number: the term *puruṣa-bahutva* (lit. 'the many-ness of consciousness') (PYŚ 2.22) indicates that consciousness exists in plural forms. This is a different presentation of consciousness than that of the nondual Vedānta ontology with which the *Gītā* becomes associated.

What else are we told about the nature of pure consciousness? It is transcendent, being eternal, unchanging and outside of space and time. And yet, consciousness is not a singular event; as noted, it is plural and infinite in number. Hence, there are as many individual consciousnesses as people who have ever lived and ever will live. The principle of reincarnation means that a consciousness is assigned to multiple human beings successively until the liberated state is reached, which brings incarnation to a halt. If these countless *puruṣa*s are not part of a singular unitary (universal) consciousness, how then are these multiple consciousnesses differentiated from each other and where do they reside (if not in space)? Multiple consciousnesses exist in the unseen dimension of reality that is non-material, but in their uniqueness and distinctiveness each consciousness is simply a witnessing presence or potential perspective within reality.

Such claims for a plurality of consciousnesses are in accord with Sāṃkhya ontology. The *Sāṃkhyakārikā* argues that consciousness is plural because if that were not the case, then everything that happened in the world would affect every individual consciousness at once. Such coincidence and simultaneity is clearly counter-rational to the sensory perception of individuated and separate human experiences of birth and death (SK 15). While in agreement with Sāṃkhya, the Pātañjala understandings of both consciousness and mind are counterposed to Buddhist ideas. One passage in the *Yogasūtra* refutes the Buddhist notion of *vijñāna*,[5] which for Buddhists can signify consciousness or thought.[6] At the close of PYŚ 3.14, in a defence of why *dharmin* (individuated substance) must be accepted as the permanent and underlying substance behind any entity (*dharma*),[7] Patañjali refutes the Buddhist arguments on this point. If, as the Buddhists maintain, each entity (*dharma*) is separate, distinct and momentary, then this too would apply to the mind, and how could experiential interaction between minds and beings be accounted for, or how could memory and recognition operate in a person if there were not an underlying mental substrate? (PYŚ 3.14) This argument underlines that although consciousness is plural in instantiation, mind is, in fact, a singular phenomenon, pertaining as it does to the substratum of *prakṛti* and evidenced by collective mental recognition and experience. The basic point here is that although there is a shared and social aspect to the mind (such as common concepts or language itself), there is a dimension of self (i.e. consciousness) which is utterly unique to the individual and almost impossible to reach through our standard cognitive apparatus. Only special forms of structured rational reflection (such as the Sāṃkhya method) can lead us there.

Freedom, disembodiment and death

For scholars (both historical and contemporary) the degree of dispassionate relation between consciousness and the material self is a topic of dispute. What exactly does disengagement with the material self mean? How can one look upon one's own mind from a detached witnessing standpoint? Interpretations of ontological disengagement range widely: periods of profound trance-like states in which cognition appears to stop, altered states of consciousness that access rare types of cognitive perception, a permanent affective shift in everyday awareness and mental operation, or the death of the physical body.

A practical interpretation of the radically liberated state of self veers away from the reading of physical death. Firstly, we have a clear indication in the commentary to YS 1.2 as to how to interpret the key maxim that mental activity should stop in yoga (*yogaś cittavṛttinirodhaḥ*):

> Because [the *sūtra*] does not say 'all' [the fluctuations stop], cognitive (*saṃprajñata*)[concentration] is also perceived to be yoga.
>
> (PYŚ 1.2)

Here, the mind does not cease functioning entirely and certainly does not cease to exist; rather, what is indicated is that particular, even most, mental processes are inhibited during profound concentration. And yet the argument that spiritual liberation is equivalent to physical death is not without foundation. In the archaic Vedic Hindu worldview and in Jainism as a whole, the notion of physical death as liberation was a common understanding. For early Vedic adepts, death with sufficient merit led to a time-limited residence in heaven.[8] For Jains, all forms of action were morally dubious and so only the end of action – strictly speaking, death – could bring about spiritual liberation. For Jains, the individuated self (*jīvātman*) was bound to the material body and could only attain liberation (*mokṣa*) at the point of the dissolution of that body, i.e. death. Even the Brahmanic ascetic followers of Śiva, the Pāśupatas, advocated that only after a long life of arduous yogic asceticism, could liberation be attained at the moment of death. This method is explained in the *c.* second century CE treatise the *Pāśupatasūtra*. However, by the fourth century, the theory of liberation-as-death had begun to fade out in favour of both the notion of embodied liberation (as evidenced in the burgeoning Buddhist concept of the *bodhisattva*, an awakened being who remained embodied in order to teach others) and in newly forming Hindu ideas about liberation-while-living, *jīvanmukti*. Also important at this time were emerging 'rapid' or subitist methods to free the self, as evidenced in the *Bhagavad Gītā*, in which Krishna's divine grace can grant sudden liberation to the devotee, without the need for a lifetime of arduous ascetic practice.

There is an association of liberation and disembodiment in Patañjali's text and, certainly, some of the framings of this notion are metaphysical. The commentary to YS 1.19 tells us that both the bodiless (*videha*) gods (*devas*) and those 'dissolved in materiality' (*prakṛtilāya*) experience a state that is akin to isolated or pure consciousness (*kaivalya*). It is unclear quite what class of beings those described as *prakṛtilāya* refers to, but presumably, in contrast to gods, they are humans and most likely the advanced meditation practioners of the text. YS 3.26 tells us further that both this group and the gods can *for a time* remain in liberation (*mokṣa*) and not function in the current world – suggesting that for humans, liberation can be a temporary state of disembodiment. YS 3.43 adds that cognitive function (*vṛtti*), when it detaches from intentional content can become greatly disembodied (*mahāvideha*). The commentary explains that *dhāraṇā* or 'fixation' is a type of disembodiment (*videha*) in which the mind functions outside of the body. This disembodiment is evident in two ways: a more ordinary state of dissociation from the empirical world and a great disembodiment which is linked to entering the bodies or minds of others. Moreover, disembodied sense capacities can cognize any object in space and time (PYŚ 3.48). This great disembodiment seems linked to the context of extraordinary mental capacities rather than final liberation. We can suggest here that dissolution in materiality (*prakṛtilāya*) can be an intermediary state towards ultimate freedom or *mokṣa*, which may be practised by yogins and other beings, and refers to a dissolution in but also a control over materiality itself, in which one can apprehend space and its objects without any restriction. It seems plausible, then, to interpret the text as outlining two forms of liberation: fleeting states of liberation during meditation in which there appears to be disembodiment and a final liberation that comes only when one's physical body dies and reincarnation has come to an end.

In the *Pātañjalayogaśāstra*, the statement on final liberation advises that the standard functioning of the mind must conclude:

> Because the mind whose function has come to an end ceases together with those predispositions (*saṃskāras*) that are conducive to isolation (*kaivalya*), *puruṣa*, now steadfast in only its own form, is solely (*kevala*) pure and is said to be liberated.
>
> (PYŚ 1.51)

Elsewhere, we are told that liberation is simply the cessation of the mind (*cittanivṛttir eva mokṣaḥ*; PYŚ 2.24). But how are we to practically understand the mind that has come to an end? PYŚ 2.10 provides some further detail. Although there are many stages that precede this (such as the elimination of the mental afflictions, or *kleśa*s), 'when the performative function of the yogin's mind dissolves, by this alone is reversal achieved' (PYŚ 2.10). The reversal here is the material process of dissolving back into primordial stasis (*mūlaprakṛti* = *pradhāna*/*aliṅga*). Furthermore, liberation is permanent (and not a transitory or repeated process): once *buddhi* has eliminated nescience or cognitive error (*adarśana*) and acquired correct perception, awareness (*buddhi*) will not arise (manifest again) since liberation is achieved (PYŚ 2.24).[9] Freedom is a state in which one's material identity, including the mind, returns to a potential form in which there is no executive function or action. If not physical death, then it is a state that is closely related, a kind of extreme dispassion towards life.

In order to better understand the relevance of death to liberation, we must incorporate the theory of moral retribution, or *karma*. According to this theory (firmly established since the late Vedic Upaniṣads), the outcome of one's death was conditioned by what one's karmic record carried, i.e. the balance sheet of merit and demerit. Without liberation, death was merely a gateway to further embodied states of lived delusion and suffering (known as *saṃsāra*, the continuous round of rebirths). Therefore, the fact of physical death was an entailment for ultimate liberation.

Yet in places, strategically perhaps, the *Yogasūtra* also pivots towards a core promise of embodied liberation. Let us briefly step back from pure subjectivity to briefly consider the social subject of the text. Patañjali's text was, after all, addressed to Brahmin males (PYŚ 2.30, PYŚ 4.29), and therefore to individuals who engaged in forms of negotiated or moderated asceticism, rather than full-blown renunciation of society (like Jain or Buddhist ascetics). Patañjali's philosophical system was also grappling with religio-social ideology that steered it away from a goal of final liberation as physical death. The cessation of the physical self (which Bronkhorst calls the ideology of cessation) (2011) is a commitment that was foregrounded by Jainism and to a lesser extent Buddhism, which are both renouncer traditions (meaning that, as a monastic, one renounces society and one's inherited social self). However, Patañjali's text, despite being clearly influenced by both Buddhism and Jainism, was formulated as a Brahmanic-Hindu text, for which the role of the householder was central. For example, Brahmin ascetics often remained married (although with limited marital duties) (Olivelle 2011: 163). Therefore, embodied existence could not be completely over-ridden by Patañjali without heed of the social implications.

The overall idea in Pātañjala yoga is the death of ordinary awareness and the ability to contemplate the self in profound ways that produce incremental dispassion from mundane life and its problems. Although designed as a method to overcome nescience, Patañjali's system also addresses the existential problem so frequently discussed by the Buddhists – that of suffering. Whereas nescience misrecognizes happiness in suffering, '[t]he discriminating one sees all as suffering' (PYŚ 2.15). Hence the suffering or pain of the human condition is based in nescience or delusion. Dispassion may offer a way to live that reduces the burden of everyday life by practising detachment. Hence the contemplative technique leads to a dispassionate awareness such as 'This does not matter to me because I am not matter, and I am therefore unaffected by this experience/person/occurrence'. From a contemporary perspective, such an instruction may appear to be both welcome and absurd. On the one hand, it can be claimed that such techniques are effective in reducing the psychological stresses of everyday encounters and offer a constructive framework to deal with the ills of modernity, such as overuse of technology. On the other hand, such techniques may be dismissed as appropriate only for privileged individuals who are not subjected to daily assaults on their embodied identities on grounds such as race or sexuality (see also 'Chapter 7: Ethics'). And yet in Patañjali's ontology, existential liberation is an even more radical affair. When still in the throes of embodied and active life, it is difficult to envisage one's own self as a pure consciousness that engages in a seeing in which there are no more objects (PYŚ 2.23) or as a floating consciousness that has no interest or engagement in anything outside of itself. Ultimate liberation framed in this way seems to be a solipsistic state, not particularly desirable or useful for a modern sensibility.

For the above reasons, I argue that the *Pātañjalayogaśāstra* offers not only the final liberation of a fully disembodied consciousness, but also temporary states of disconnection from mundane existence during deep contemplation. In these meditative states, one can transcend mundane awareness and see one's own material identity (as a mind-body complex) from the perspective of consciousness. Patanjali's yogic philosophy, then, is a technique of self-consciousness. Liberation (*hāna*, or the escape from *saṃsāra*) is simply the means of having correct perception or knowledge (*samyagdarśana*) of reality (PYŚ 2.15), which is the capacity to see the world and self for what they are. But 'seeing' or 'knowing' the self is not in itself a sufficient condition for freedom; freedom also requires an ontological transformation.

The sevenfold model of wisdom (*prajñā*) outlined at PYŚ 2.27 demonstrates a combination of epistemological and ontological freedoms and the sequential relationship between the two. The first four stages are framed primarily in terms of the knowledge to be gained and the last three in terms of the changes to one's state of being.

Pātañjala yoga is a self-centred technique in that the contemplative method is one of self-enquiry: gaining knowledge about the self by

Table 2 Patañjali's seven stages of wisdom (*Pātañjalayogaśāstra*, 2.27). © Karen O'Brien-Kop.

1	What is to be escaped has been fully examined.	*parijñātaṃ heyaṃ nāsya punaḥ parijñeyam asti*	Fourfold freedom from knowledge of anything left to be done
2	The causes of what is to be escaped have dwindled and do not need to be destroyed.	*kṣīṇā heyahetavo na punar eteṣāṃ kṣetavyam asti.*	
3	Abandonment by means of *nirodhasamādhi*.	*nirodhasamādhinā hānam.*	
4	Perfection of discriminating perception.	*bhāvito vivekakhyātirūpo hānopāya iti.*	
5	Buddhi has completed its function.	*caritādhikārā buddhiḥ.*	Threefold freedom of the mind
6	The *guṇa*s turn towards dissolution (like rocks falling from a mountain) and along with them comes everything else. The *guṇa*s, dissolved, do not reappear.	*guṇā giriśikharataṭacyutā iva grāvāṇo niravasthānāḥ svakāraṇe pralayābhimukhāḥ saha tenāstaṃ gacchanti.na caiṣāṃ pravilīnānāṃ punar asty utpādaḥ prayojanābhāvād iti.*	
7	In the state beyond the *guṇa*s, *puruṣa* is solitary and self-illuminating.	*etasyām avasthāyāṃ guṇasaṃbandhātītaḥ svarūpamātrajyotir amalaḥ kevalī puruṣa iti.*	

using the self as the means to do so. Hence, one cited verse explains that yoga itself is the instructor of yoga:

> 'Yoga is to be known by means of yoga.
> Yoga comes into being due to yoga.
> One who, by means of yoga, is attentive
> Abides in yoga for a long time'.
>
> (PYŚ 3.6)

How does the higher-functioning mind (*buddhi*) begin to observe and become aware of its own machinations? Patañjali tells us that there are two types of entities (*dharmas*) in the mind (*citta*):[10] those that are directly seen/perceived (*paridṛṣṭa*) and those that cannot be directly perceived (*aparidṛṣṭa*) (PYŚ 3.15). Whereas ideation (*pratyaya*) belongs to the former category of the directly perceptible, the substantially real (*vastumātra*) or true objects in the mind cannot be directly perceived (like the distinction between the *dharma* and the *dharmin*, the object and its substance that we discussed in 'Chapter 2: Metaphysics'). These invisible aspects of the mind are enumerated as sevenfold: cessation (*nirodha*), virtue (*dharma*),[11] predisposition (*saṃskāra*), change (*pariṇāma*), life (*jīva*), action (*ceṣṭā*) and power/capacity (*śakti*) (PYŚ 3.15). These seven features of mind cannot be perceived, but are only to be known by means of inference (*anumāna*). This theory has prototypical resonances for modern notions of the subconscious or unconscious (see 'Chapter 4: Epistemology' for a discussion of inference).

And what of cognition of death? Although death is the impetus that makes the wheel of *saṃsāra* go round (producing endless cycles of transmigration), any conviction in the reality of death itself is a cognitive error. As PYŚ 2.9 explains to us, the affliction or misconception known as fear of death (*abhiniveśa*) is a grand illusion. The text notes that it is commonly reasoned that death could only be feared if it were real. Although fear of death manifests in every creature as the instinct of self-preservation, the text reminds us that such fear is incompatible with the metaphysics of yoga. Even though it undergoes change, transformation and even dissolution, material never 'dies', but rather returns to its primordial state (*pradhāna* = *mūlaprakṛti*/*aliṅga*/*avyakta*). Equally, consciousness never dies since it is eternal. Hence the immortality of both the conscious self (*puruṣa*) and the material self (when it returns to *prakṛti*) is confirmed (PYŚ 2.9).

The timeless self

So where do these discussions leave the self? We should by now be clear that true subjectivity is timeless.

> The active power of consciousness does not transform, has no intermixture, is pure when objects are shown to it, and is eternal.
>
> (PYŚ 1.2)

The many techniques of reflection and meditation in the *Yogasūtra* are designed to practically direct awareness to this profound realization:

> When proficiency in non-apprehending (*nirvicāra*) concentration arises, then the yogin becomes the clarified supreme self (*adhyātma*) whose object is true reality, and the sphere of wisdom (*prajñā*) is expanded beyond time (*krama*).
>
> (PYŚ 1.47)

The theory of the true self reflects the theory of time as eternal, in that the permanent watchful self (pure consciousness) observes the changing states of the material-corporeal-mental self, knowing that it is ontologically 'real' (as *prakṛti*) but not 'true' (as is *puruṣa*). One also learns that the material self appears subject to change but will ultimately dissolve in the ground of being, space and time and that the ultimate dissolution cannot take place until the ethical debts of *karma* have been eradicated.

Discussion questions

1. What do you understand to be the difference, if any, between awareness and consciousness?
2. The *Yogasūtra* reasons that consciousness endures after physical death – are you aware of other reasoned arguments or empirical studies that make this same claim convincingly?
3. What is your assessment of Patañjali's theory of existential freedom, and do you have other favoured theories that you argue for?

Further reading

Bronkhorst, J. (2011) *Karma*. Honolulu: University of Hawaii Press.

Burley, M. (2007) *Classical Sāṃkhya and Yoga: An Indian Metaphysics of Experience*. London and New York: Routledge.

Frazier, J. (2014) 'Introduction: The Importance of "Thinking Inside the Box"' in Frazier, J. (ed.) *Categorisation in Indian Philosophy: Thinking inside the Box*. London and New York: Routledge.

Gokhale, P. (2020) *The Yogasūtra of Patañjali: A New Introduction to the Buddhist Roots of the Yoga System*. Delhi: Routledge India.

Larson, G. (2018) 'Introduction' in *Classical Yoga Philosophy and the Legacy of Sāṃkhya with Sanskrit Text and English Translation of Pātañjala* Yogasūtra-*s*, Vyāsa Bhāṣya *and* Tattvavaiśāradī *of Vācaspatimiśra*. (MLBD Classical Systems of Indian Philosophy: 2) Delhi: Motilal Banarsidass.

Larson, G. and Bhattacharya, R. S. (eds.) (2008) *Yoga: India's Philosophy of Meditation*. Volume 12 *Encyclopedia of Indian Philosophies*. Delhi: Motilal Banarsidass Publishers Private Ltd.

Rukmani, T. S. (2011) 'Sāṃkhya-Yoga' in Edelglass, W. and Garfield, J. (eds.) *The Oxford Handbook of World Philosophy*. Oxford: Oxford University Press.

4

Epistemology: The primacy of perception

Chapter outline

Early Brahmanic-Hindu epistemology was constrained by metaphysics. Hence the nature of reality and the possibilities of knowledge were determined by the ideas and content of the Vedas. However, as philosophical knowledge was codified through the genre of *śāstra*, epistemology began to take on a life of its own, separate from religious knowledge. New and systematized answers were developed to answer the old questions, such as: What is the nature of knowledge? How does one know something to be true? What are the instruments of knowledge? We can say that all of the early schools (discussed in 'Chapter 1: Introduction'), both *āstika* and *nāstika,* were motivated by a concern with epistemology and the existential problems caused by incorrect knowledge and nescience (*avidyā*). Since it is faulty knowledge (of the self, of reality) that produces misperception and hence suffering, the schools engage in methods and principles to distinguish correct from incorrect knowledge. In Early Indian Philosophy, the practical goal of theoretical reasoning was liberation, liberation from the imprisonment of false knowledge. Hence, epistemology and logic were used to correct wrong views and to know reality accurately. The importance of knowledge in Early Indian Philosophy cannot be overstated, since it is knowledge that brings about liberation. Patañjali's understanding of bondage was that it occurred through the mind; as PYŚ 2.18 makes clear, bondage exists in the mind alone, specifically in *buddhi*'s failure to recognize the purpose of consciousness. The mind, therefore, is also the site where liberation is initiated.[1]

The purpose of consciousness is knowing

There is no avoiding epistemology in any understanding of Pātañjala yoga, since it is a system whose end goal is a state of pure and objectless consciousness, a non-cognitive state of knowing. Although in 'Chapter 3: Ontology' we discussed consciousness and materiality as both co-fundamental and co-ultimate, the privileged point of existence is undoubtedly contentless consciousness (*puruṣa*) and not the material content of life (*prakṛti*). What is the nature of this knowing? YS 4.34 explains the abiding of the power of consciousness (*citśakti*) in its own form. This means that the knowledge that exists in consciousness is not of the material world, but of one's own nature as pure consciousness. This is not to say that a liberated *puruṣa* does not witness the world – indeed a synonym for *puruṣa* is *kṣetrajña*, the knower of the field (PYŚ 2.15) – but the nature of this knowing is passive witnessing, and there is no attachment, not even to an embodied self.

In Yoga, as in Sāṃkhya, there is a distinction between consciousness and the mind. In order to prevent any confusion, I reserve the term consciousness for *puruṣa* alone. This is distinct from the mind complex, which belongs to the realm of materiality, and which can be associated with terms like 'awareness', 'thinking', 'mentality', 'rationality', 'intelligence' and so on, but never with consciousness. Consciousness is not a property of *prakṛti*, and since the mind resides in the domain of *prakrti*, neither can the mind be equated with consciousness. This may seem counterintuitive to a contemporary sensibility in which 'mind' and 'consciousness' are quite entangled. Moreover, an increasingly universalized discourse of public mental health has gradually become dominated by technical terms in Buddhist meditation, such as mindfulness, awareness and awakening, which can sometimes be conflated with consciousness. But for us to understand the Sāṃkhya-Yoga philosophy of mind, we need to separate out the term 'consciousness' (as the method itself invites).

Consciousness is non-intentional in that it has no content and no objects of cognition. Neither can it be cognized as an object – in short, it is not of the objective world (*prakṛti*) and represents a pure subjectivity. The *Sāṃkhyakārikā* is illuminating on this point:

> And thus, due to [its being] the opposite [of *prakṛti*], the witnessing, aloneness, equanimity, awareness and inactivity of *puruṣa* is established.
>
> (SK 19; trs. Burley 2007: 168)

Puruṣa's status here as inactive and equanimous signals that it does not undergo any change. It is what we might call a pure witnessing presence – forever seeing, but never engaging or being perturbed, since it is only the act of perceiving without any content. *Prakṛti* on the other hand is devoid of consciousness, is the 'stuff' of life and of the world, and is constantly generating, changing and dissolving forms.

Although it can be risky (i.e. reductive) to describe the *puruṣa-prakṛti* relation as that of subject-object, this is an ever-lingering implication of the dualist metaphysics and ontology. Yet the overarching frame also suggests a subject-subject relation. SK 21, which refers to 'the blind' and 'the lame', alludes to this, in that one cannot proceed without the other.[2] But nonetheless, in a system that values knowledge, it is consciousness (i.e. pure subjectivity) that is the prime principle, technically. This is because, as Chakrabarti puts it:

> There can be no object without consciousness, that is, nothing can be cognized without consciousness. At the same time, there can be no object without the subject, that is, nothing can be cognized without the subject. Thus the pure subject presupposed by each and every object is pure consciousness.
>
> (Chakrabarti 1999: 182)

We can also add here that although the primacy of consciousness as the only site of true cognition hints at an epistemological idealism, nonetheless it is epistemological realism that prevails, since *prakṛti* exists eternally independently of consciousness. (See also discussion of idealism in 'Chapter 2: Metaphysics'.)

The valid bases of knowledge

Indian philosophical thought at the time of the *Yogasūtra* held to a framework of threefold perception (*triputī pratyakṣa*): the subject which knows (*pramāta*), the object which is known (*prameya*) and the process of knowing (*pramiti*).[3] The *Yogasūtra* uses the Sāṃkhya terms 'seer' (*draṣṭṛ*), the 'seen' (*dṛśya*) and the process of 'seeing' (*darśana*) (e.g. PYŚ 2.6; PYŚ 2.17,[4] 2.18[5]). Patañjali's text also has its own terms for this model, drawn from 'grasping' (verbal root √*gṛh*): 'perceiver' (*grahītṛ*), 'perceived object' (*grāhya*) and process of 'perceiving' (*grahaṇa*) (YS 1.41). Beyond this shared tripartite model, and as part of increasing systematization of philosophy, the Indian schools of thought developed a shared set of six valid bases of knowledge (*pramāṇa*s). These are perception, inference, reliable testimony (or authority), analogy (or comparison), postulation (or presumption) and non-cognition. Although different philosophical schools sometimes used variant technical terms to describe these modes and to further refine them, they are more or less a staple of philosophical reasoning during the period of the *sūtras* and *śāstras* and endure until the present day. To describe these modes or bases of knowledge concisely:

Perception (*pratyakṣa*) is the most important of all the *pramāṇas*. It is the means of direct and immediate knowledge. Perception is not dependent on any other *pramāṇa*, but they are all dependent on it:

> the primacy of direct perception cannot be defeated by a different form of valid knowledge (*pramāṇa*). Indeed, the use of a different form of valid knowledge is obtained only by the power of direct perception.
> (PYŚ 1.32)[6]

Inference (*anumāna*) is a process by which one proposition is arrived at and affirmed on the basis of another proposition. This is also called reasoning.

Reliable testimony or authority (*āgama/śabda/śruta*) refers to the textual authority of the Vedas or the authority of a teacher (*guru*), i.e. a reliable witness.

Analogy or comparison (*upamāna*) is knowledge that is derived from an example that is similar.

Postulation or presumption (*arthāpatti*) is knowledge that is only intelligible by assuming something else.

Non-cognition (*anupalabdhi*) can take different forms such as an intuitive flash or burst of knowledge or, indeed, knowledge that cognizes what is absent or non-existent.

Each school defined its identity, in part, by the valid bases (or means) of knowledge that it accepted. And later Indian scholars grouped or paired schools according to which *pramāṇas* they accepted. For example, the philosophical systems that adhered to perception, inference and analogy as the only valid means of knowledge were certain sub-schools of Vedānta (Viśiṣṭādvaita Vedānta and Dvaita Vedānta). For the Vaiśeṣikas and most Buddhist schools, only perception and inference were accepted.[7] Nyāya extended its *pramāṇas* to include perception, inference, testimony and analogy – while Prabhākara

Mīmāṃsā adhered to these four, plus a fifth, postulation. At the extreme ends of the *pramāṇa* debates were the Cārvākas (materialists), a little understood school today, who accepted only perception and rejected all other bases, while the subschools Advaita Vedānta and Bhāṭṭa Mīmāṃsā accepted all six options for attaining valid knowledge.

The pairing of the Yoga school with Sāṃkhya was made on several counts, such as metaphysics and a shared method of rational reflection. But one further factor that connected these two systems was the acceptance by both of three valid bases of knowledge: perception, inference and authority (also shared, on the whole, by the Jains). Let us briefly visit the common understanding of the *pramāṇa*s between Pātañjala yoga and Īśvarakṛṣṇa's Sāṃkhya – and some vital differences. Perception and authority will be discussed in this chapter, while inference is considered in 'Chapter 5: Logic'. Authority is further discussed in 'Chapter 6: Philosophy of Language'.

The primacy of perception

Perception was generally described by early Indian philosophers as being of two types: determinate (*savikalpaka*) and indeterminate (*nirvikalpaka*). As with the valid bases of knowledge, individual schools took up their own stance on the validity of this distinction. On the whole, Nyāya, Vaiśeṣika, Sāṃkhya, Yoga and Mīmāṃsā asserted that determinate and indeterminate perception were linked thus: first there is an indeterminate perception of an object, a kind of immediate or raw apprehension with no distinct qualities apparent (like blurry vision), which is followed by determinate perception of the object, as generic and specific qualities swim into focus. Other schools, however, disagreed. Advaitins argued that determinate and indeterminate perceptions were not, in fact, part of a continuum but were rather separate and unrelated types. Jains and certain Vedāntins (Dvaita and Viśiṣṭādvaita) rejected indeterminate perception as possible at all. Elsewhere, the Buddhists' theory of ontological flux led to a rebuff of the claim that determinate perception was possible. There is also an important point in these theories about true and false perception: at the level of indeterminate perception in which there is a collection of qualities (particulars but also universals) that are not yet properly linked, processed or digested into a 'whole', there can be no judgement of true or false. It is only at the level of determinate cognition that truth value can be ascertained.

Pātañjala yoga, like Sāṃkhya, adhered to a theory of direct realism – that reality can be directly perceived as it is, and that the raw data of sense perception (particulars) create whole or universal objects that can be directly perceived as things in themselves (without a constructive or distorting role for conceptual overlay). The only exception to this is the cognitive fault of existential misperception – of mistaking materiality for consciousness. Perception (by which is often meant 'direct perception' or seeing with one's own eyes) brings particulars into focus:

> The *pramāṇa* called direct perception (*pratyakṣa*) is the mental process (*vṛtti*) that is caused by contact with external objects through the channel of the senses. The object is characterized by the universal and the particular, but direct perception focuses on the particular.
>
> (PYŚ 1.7)

However, even if perception illuminates particulars, the *Pātañjalayogaśāstra* is keen to emphasize the reality of the 'true object' as a whole, even if understood as a conglomeration of atomic parts (PYŚ 1.43).[8] (See also 'Chapter 2: Metaphysics'.) This point is maintained in order to avoid any confusion with the position of the Buddhists for whom only indeterminate perception was real (because there are no fixed features or qualities in reality to see in a determinate way). For Patañjali, the Buddhist claim is absurd because it lacks any firm ground for true knowledge of objects as 'whole':

> However, for one [i.e. a Buddhist] who [sees] the collection of particulars as devoid of an objective referent, [for whom] the subtle cause is absent, there is false knowledge because of non-perception of the whole [object] established in its own form without linguistic/conceptual construction (*avikalpa*) – then, for the most part, only false

> knowledge of everything is obtained. If the object is non-existent, what then would be right knowledge? Whatever is perceivable is known by means of being whole.
>
> (PYŚ 1.43)

The role of perception, according to Patañjali, is to see reality as it is, i.e. to see true objects in their whole form.

Yogic perception (*yogipratyakṣa*)

However, perception was not restricted to sensory perception. Most schools, including Nyāya and certain Buddhist approaches, accept a special type of perception that is attained only by *yogin*s (adepts/followers of a yoga system) and associated with the extraordinary (*alaukika*) – such as seeing the future, or observing details that are atomic in size. Yet there is a tension in how these supersensory capacities are described, since they are ultimately classed as distractions to the goal of liberation (YS 3.37). There is also a dialectic in the text between these forms of perception as supernatural and as subtle rational functions: for example, the claim that the yogin can see into other minds (YS 3.19) is qualified in the very next *sūtra* as a general kind of capacity in which common ideas can be recognized, but not the specific subjective contents of another's mind in relation to object referents (YS 3.20). This is a mundane explanation for what might otherwise be construed as a supernatural power. Elsewhere, yogic perception that is classed as extraordinary (*alaukika*) perception includes a technical analysis of cognition, such as seeing a universal 'cowness' instantiated every time one perceives a cow, or having relational knowledge arise even if it is not perceived (such as seeing snow and perceiving the relational quality of 'cold' even without touching it). Another type of perception that is particular to the yogis is *jyotiṣmatī* (YS 1.36; PYŚ 3.25), a type of perceptive illumination that reveals subtle, hidden or remote facets of reality, again suggesting an extraordinary sharpness, range and depth to the perceptive mind engaged in this philosophical pursuit.

A more ordinary way of understanding yogic perception, however, is simply as a type of perception cultivated in practice, i.e. steady and uninterrupted for long periods. As PYŚ 3.2 tells us, the state of absorption (*dhyāna*) is the capacity to perceive an object steadily so as to produce a continuous stream of focused thought, such that no other thought interferes with or intercepts this process. Once this skill is established, one can then attain perfected and one-pointed concentration (*samādhi*). There is in this perfected concentration (of the objective sort) a non-dual relation with the object, i.e. an identity of knowledge and thing in a relation that is 'true'. PYŚ 3.3 spells out this state for us as one in which all conceptuality or ideation has been emptied out of the perception so that there is only pure knowledge of the 'thing-in-itself', the true object. The perception of materiality as it truly exists is a desired state, since, ultimately, it is correct knowledge of materiality (and its separation from consciousness) that leads to liberation. Patañjali's definition of yogic perception is picked up on by later Buddhist philosophers such as Dignāga (fifth–sixth century CE) and Dharmakīrti (*c.* seventh century CE) (Dunne 2007).

Perception and truth

The goal of concentration (*samādhi*) is to attain wisdom or insight (*prajñā*) that is truth-bearing (*ṛtaṃbharā*) (PYŚ 1.48). The nature of a mind that can perceive the truth is transparent luminosity, i.e. truth is self-evident and is simply revealed by the light of sattvic *buddhi* (in the case of the 'true object') or the light or *puruṣa* (in the case of the 'true subject or self'). A further characteristic of truth-bearing knowledge is its apprehension of the particular:

> [it] has a different object than that arising from the wisdom (*prajñā*) of authority (*śruta*) and inference (*anumāṇa*) due to the particularity of the object.
>
> (YS 1.49)

We have already been told (discussed above) that only perception can ascertain the particulars of an object, and so the equivalence is made between truth-bearing insight (*ṛtaṃbharā prajñā*) and direct perception, the most prized basis of knowledge. This is an important point in understanding the ontology and epistemology of the *Yogasūtra*: while authoritative scripture or instruction and philosophical reasoning (inference within logic; argumentation) can give us access to universals, only perception can give us access to particulars and only knowledge that includes particulars is true knowledge. This relates both to knowledge of the object (in order to see it as a thing in itself) and of the subject (to realize one's own individuated consciousness).

Testimony or authority

A key discussion of testimony or authority occurs in the description of the nature of *īśvara* (the lord). The questions are posed as to how *īśvara*'s eminence is proved, reasoned or caused:

> Is the eternal eminence of *īśvara*, which arises from the cause of his superior *sattva*, with proof or without proof? Its proof is *śāstra*. And what is the proof of *śāstra*? The proof of [his] superior *sattva*. Both the *śāstra* and the eminence, residing in *īśvara*'s *sattva*, are in a perpetual relationship [without beginning or end].
>
> (PYŚ 1.24)

The reasoning here is cyclical: the proof of *īśvara* is in the authoritative scriptures and treatises (such as the Vedas), and the cause of such scripture is *īśvara*. These statements do not sit neatly with our understanding of *īśvara* as a special *puruṣa* (see 'Chapter 2: Metaphysics'), since language then would be an exceptional phenomenon associated both with consciousness and with materiality. Rather, the framing of *īṣvara* at PYŚ 1.24 appears to sit within a more archaic Vedic worldview. What is clear from the passage, however, is the sealing of scripture as a linguistic emanation from the divine realm rather than any human author. Scripture, after all, is *śruti* or 'heard' by humans, i.e. revealed to them, rather than composed by authors. This lends a certain infallibility to scripture, which is why some schools rejected it as a valid basis of knowledge. The *Pātañjalayogaśāstra* acknowledges that in cases such as theistic knowledge, there are limitations on the types of *pramāṇa*s that can be employed. Since inference is most effective in determining universals, its application in determining the particular qualities of *īśvara* is ineffective (PYŚ 1.25). Furthermore, *īśvara* cannot be directly perceived. Therefore valid knowledge about *īśvara* can only be based on authority, in this case scripture (*āgama*) (PYŚ 1.25).

In the case of the objective world, however, the primacy of perception prevails. Scriptural authority and inference have their roles to play in obtaining knowledge, but nonetheless direct perception is always the best means,

> even if the true nature of real-world objects (*arthatattva*) is also obtained by the instruction of a teacher, inference, and *śāstra*. Even though from the capacity of instruction the true essence of these [objects is known], as long as even one part is not known directly by a person, so is the whole out of sight; i.e. the entire awareness (*buddhi*) does not apprehend subtle objects, such as liberation (*apavarga*) and so forth. Therefore, for the sake of confirming the instruction of the teacher, inference, and the *śāstra*, some particular quality of the object must inevitably be known by an eye-witness (*pratyākṣin*).
>
> (PYŚ 1.35)

To have a firm conviction about the reality of liberation, the most effective basis of valid knowledge will be to glimpse reality for oneself.

To sum up: there is no tension in the *pramāṇa*s between how cognitions come into being and how they are shown to be valid; that is to say, the concept of *pramāṇa* includes both of these points. As Gupta explains: 'The *pramāṇa*s are both instruments by which cognitions arise, as well as the ways of justifying a cognitive claim' (Gupta 2012: 13).

The perils of nescience

There are several terms used to refer to nescience or false knowledge. One is *mithyājñāna* (wrong knowledge; PYŚ 2.26); another is *adarśana*, meaning non-sight (e.g. PYŚ 2.23), and perhaps the most commonly used is *avidyā* (ignorance, nescience).

Adarśana (non-seeing) is a negated term (*a-darśana*). The word for correct knowledge (*darśana*) is the same as the word for 'seeing' or 'sight of' (and is also an equivalent Sanskrit term for 'philosophy'). Hence, *darśana* is the enemy of *adarśana* (PYŚ 2.23), i.e. 'seeing' is the enemy of 'non-seeing'. Indeed, the commentarial passage on YS 2.23 continues with a fascinating summary of the orthodox views on how exactly the word *adarśana* should be understood, according to the mainstream philosophical tracts (*śāstras*). *Adarśana* can be defined or further explained as follows. *Adarśana* is:

- When the *guṇas* (material qualities) are functioning or interacting
- The non-appearance of the mind to consciousness
- Due to the purpose (goal) of the *guṇas* (i.e. material emanation)
- Understood as nescience (*avidyā*), it is eradicated when the mind dissolves along with all seeds of future arising of mind
- The existence of active mental predispositions (*saṃskāras*) due to the destruction of tranquil predispositions
- Due to the fact that the purpose of primordial matter (*pradhāna*) is to manifest and be seen (*darśana*) – that's wrong seeing (*adarśana*)
- The non-seeing by *puruṣa* when primordial matter (*pradhāna*) exists, since there is nothing to see then (no objects in formation)
- Can be attributed to both materiality and consciousness, in that *adarśana* in the mind can also be witnessed by *puruṣa* – like any other object
- Is simply part of the knowledge derived from seeing (PYŚ 2.23)

What we notice in this list is a nuanced range of meanings for 'non-seeing', most of which refer to nescience as the existential problem of wrong knowledge, but some of which are more neutrally descriptive or even positive.

In contrast to the three valid bases of knowledge outlined at YS 1.7, YS 1.8–9 explains false knowledge (*mithyājñāna*) as erroneous cognition or illusion (see also PYŚ 2.26). Indeed PYŚ 1.8 explains that false knowledge is fivefold and is the formula known as the mental afflictions (*kleśa*s): nescience (*avidyā*), egoity (*asmitā*), attachment (*rāga*), aversion (*dveṣa*) and fear of death (*abhiniveśa*). Since nescience (*avidyā*) is the basis of the five afflictions, the other four are forms of false knowledge that spring from it (YS 2.4). That the afflictions are more cognitive than affective is evident in the clarification that they are also to be known as the absence of perception: hence equivalent to the five states of darkness, delusion, great confusion, great darkness and total darkness (*tamas, moha, mahāmoha, tāmisra, andhatāmisra*) (PYŚ 1.8).[9] Moreover, PYŚ 2.3 explains that the word *kleśa* means erroneous cognitions or misconceptions (*viparyaya*), which are acquired at the time of wrong ideation (*viparyasā pratyaya*) (PYŚ 2.4). There is a correlation between the list of the five *kleśa*s and the order of the five metaphoric states of cognitive darkness. Hence the utmost level of darkness, total darkness, would be equated with the fifth affliction, fear of death. PYŚ 2.10 explains that this is a misconception rather than just a feeling state: this fear of death 'does not arise by direct perception, inference, or testimony' (PYŚ 2.10), i.e. any of the three *pramāṇa*s, because it can never belong to the realm of valid knowledge. As a lack of conviction in the immortality of consciousness (which never changes or dies), fear of death is the most extreme case of cognitive error or illusion.

Incidentally, this is the same list of five states of cognitive confusion and darkness found in the *Sāṃkhyakārikā* at SK 48. The five *kleśa*s, on the other hand, are customarily discussed in Buddhist texts. So, Patañjali appears to be conjoining two similar models of cognitive error or distortion in his synthetic philosophical project. Here, again, we see the primacy of perception as the basis of all true knowledge. Not only is true knowledge explained as illumination, but false knowledge is consistently framed as lack of ability to see accurately due to the absence of light (e.g. modes of cognitive darkness).[10]

Patañjali's second *pāda* introduces two methods that are designed to thin out and eventually eliminate the afflictions. The active method, *kriyā yoga*, attenuates the afflictions. When this process is followed by meditation techniques (e.g. *dhyāna*, *prasaṃkhyāna*) that lead to concentration (*samādhi*), even the seeds of affliction will be scorched by the fire of meditation until their germination capacity is utterly destroyed (PYŚ 2.2, 2.4, 2.10–11; PYŚ 2.26). Yet this is not an easy process. As YS 2.5 informs us, nescience (divided into the five afflictions) is also the fundamental error of:

> **[mistaking] impermanence, impurity, suffering, and non-self for permanence, purity, happiness, and perception of self.**
>
> (YS 2.5)

This argument sets up true beliefs from Sāṃkhya (e.g. that the world is permanent and there is a core self) against false doctrines from Buddhism (e.g. that the world is impermanent or that there is no fixed self) – and it is a grave mistake to mix up the two outlooks.

There is repeated analysis of the complexity of the mind and its faults as due to *karma* and nescience in which the afflictions are consistently described as *avidyā*, or *mithyājñāna* e.g. PYŚ 2.26. Mental predispositions (*saṃskāras*) formed by karmic imprints and traces are not simple in structure, but can form complex conglomerations that spread out in many directions (PYŚ 2.13). The mind (*citta*) is said to be a coagulation of various effects from multiple previous lifetimes – an entanglement of the outcomes of afflictions (*kleśas*), moral action (*karma*), moral retribution (*vipāka*), experience and memories (PYŚ 2.13). Such karmic effects develop and mature at different speeds according to kind. Hence, Patañjali's text offers a sophisticated theory of mind, not as technically detailed as some theories developed by the Buddhists, but certainly sound and in places impressive in its relevance for contemporary audiences with an interest in cognitive scientific models of mind. One commentarial passage explains the events that take place in the mind as perception (*grahaṇa*), retention (*dhāraṇā*), reasoning (*ūha*), negation (*apoha*), true knowledge (*tattvajñāna*) and clinging to life or fear of death (*abhiniveśa*) – furthermore, these are continually being observed by consciousness (PYŚ 2.18).[11]

To sum up: the two main stages in Pātañjala yoga are (1) destroying the cognitive illusions produced by the five mental afflictions (*kleśas*) so that ultimately (2) discriminating discernment, or true knowledge, can be acquired (YS 2.28).[12]

Liberating knowledge

Patañjali's system describes an ideal ontological state for any subject, a state of being that is pure knowing (and nothing else). And so in order to actualize the difference between *puruṣa* and *prakṛti* as ontological, one must begin and end with epistemology.

If *puruṣa* is consciousness, then *prakṛti* is the content of consciousness; if *puruṣa* is knowledge, then *prakṛti* (being unconscious) is therefore the site of nescience and misidentification, which takes place through the mind-complex of mundane functions (*manas*), egoity (*ahaṃkāra*) and awareness/intelligence (*buddhi*). Even in its highest and most refined state as *sattva* (the quality or *guṇa* of balance/purity), the mind is only capable of awareness (*buddhi*) and not of consciousness (*puruṣa*), which is a different, non-mental phenomenon. Moreover, only *buddhi* can possess awareness of ignorance, but *puruṣa* as the site of liberated knowledge can have no knowledge that is ignorance, since this would be a contradiction to its perfection. It can, however, be a witness to nescience that exists in the mind. This throws up at least two puzzles for getting to grips with Patañjali's liberation in a practical sense. Firstly, what is the mechanism by which liberation takes place – does it happen in *buddhi* or in *puruṣa*? Secondly, if *puruṣa* is always-already pure (free from nescience), then why does liberation need to take place at all? Fortunately, these two questions can be answered with the same explanation: liberation happens at the site of *buddhi*, when the mind recognizes itself for what it is (a material and limited entity), and this recognition recasts the centre of being from a material mind to pure consciousness, cutting the *puruṣa* free from that particular material (i.e. embodied) instantiation of self.

(A further puzzle is if this entails physical death, but I have addressed this question in 'Chapter 3: Ontology'.)

There are many nuances in Patañjali's sophisticated theory of existential freedom. Ultimately, the philosophical method of the *Yogasūtra* facilitates a means and type of liberating knowledge that is beyond subject-object dualism, i.e. pure knowledge itself is situated within a pure and unmediated subjectivity (*puruṣa*). This is not the same as transcendent knowledge, like the knowledge Arjuna experiences when he witnesses the theophany of Krishna in the *Bhagavad Gītā*, since there are certain limits in yogic epistemology.[13] If there are, as Patañjali claims, countless consciousnesses, then even liberated knowledge in this system is still deeply subjective in that it is 'located' and belongs to some 'one' individuated consciousness. It is not the dislocated, impersonal and transcendent consciousness of *brahman* in the Vedānta system. Liberating knowledge here constitutes a theory of personhood and hence entails plural outcomes for many different beings, rather than referring to a theory of a singular cosmic or metaphysical consciousness. Let us recall that there are an infinite number of *puruṣa*s that can be liberated, meaning that freedom is a variegated rather than a uniform phenomenon.

Finally, there is an inextricability between the method of knowledge and the goal of knowledge. The philosophical method is the condition that makes liberating knowledge possible, or as Mohanty puts it: '*mokṣa* is the experiential equivalent of the theoretical position of a system, or [...] the theoretical position of a system is intended to provide for the possibility of actualizing that ideal' (Mohanty 2000: 144). Hence it is, in practice, difficult to separate out the roles of epistemology, ontology and logic in achieving the ideal state of personhood that Patañjali proposes.

Cognitive and non-cognitive knowledge

The text holds a complex (perhaps even ambivalent) attitude towards cognition. Pātañjala yoga is a system of rational reflection, and yet the purpose of the yoga philosophy is to bring about the cessation of cognitive acts, or thought forms (*vṛttis*) (YS 1.2). This cessation occurs across two stages: firstly, one practises meditation on objects (cognitive or objective concentration, *saṃprajñāta samādhi*) and, secondly, one practises beyond objects (non-cognitive or non-objective concentration, *asaṃprajñāta samādhi*). The text is clear that it is only in this latter state that mundane mental processes have stopped, although some predispositions (*saṃskāras*) will remain until liberation occurs (PYŚ 1.18). Non-objective concentration is a state that is empty, void or absent of objects (PYŚ 1.18) (and is closely approaching the 'contentless' and pure state of *puruṣa*). PYŚ 3.8 tells us that the direct means to attain objective concentration is the threefold method of fixing-absorbing-concentrating the mind (*dhāraṇā, dhyāna, samādhi*). However, this is only an indirect means for non-objective (or non-cognitive) concentration, which can also take place without this sequential process. Non-cognitive concentration is the goal of meditative practice. As a state devoid of objects, it resembles consciousness. Yet *samādhi* as a process of collecting or focusing mental efforts is still associated with the mental realm rather than pure, liberated consciousness. We can therefore consider non-cognitive concentration as a threshold state or gateway to realizing *puruṣa*.

Models of mind

Interestingly, the location of higher awareness (*vijñāna*) in Patañjali's text is not associated with the brain, as we might expect from a modern perspective, but rather with the heart. By focusing on the heart (an archaic location for *brahman-ātman* in the Upaniṣads),[14] one becomes a knower of the mind itself (*cittasaṃvit*) (PYŚ 3.34). When concentrating on the heart (which is described as being a lotus flower), there is direct perception of awareness itself, *buddhi* (PYŚ 1.36). There is more than a hint here of trying to reconcile two philosophical systems: the notion of the heart as the site of *brahman* and the Sāṃkhya concept of consciousness as isolated *puruṣa*. However, no explicit attempt is made to conflate the two systems of thought.

On the whole, the mind is analysed according to Sāṃkhya ontology as a threefold structure, evolving in the order of awareness (*buddhi*), egoity (*ahaṃkāra*) and mundane processes (*manas*). Sometimes this triadic complex is referred to as *citta*, and sometimes *citta* is used as a synonym for *buddhi*.

Awareness (*buddhi*)

Awareness or *buddhi* (which is also referred to as *mahat* and *citta*) is the highest and most subtle function of mind, where perception takes place, since *buddhi* is the power of seeing (PYŚ 2.6). Let us see what we can discern about the mechanics of *buddhi*.

Buddhi is assumed to have a plasticity which means that when objects are cognized, *buddhi* assumes the form (*akāra*) of the object. Like a crystal that is coloured by whatever is proximate to it, so does *citta* (=*buddhi*) take on the form and hue of that which it perceives, be it subtle or gross (PYŚ 1.41). The modern sensibility of 'you are what you think' finds a philosophical home in Patañjali's system. The ideal and ultimate object for the mind is, of course, the always-already liberated *puruṣa* (PYŚ 1.41). Paradoxically, however, as soon as one glimpses *puruṣa* and hence becomes *puruṣa* (assumes its form and hue), then the mind is dissolved and one is freed.

But another important way in which this mental process (*vṛtti*) takes place is through the concept of reflection (*pratibimba*). Reflection seems to travel in two directions into the *buddhi* – both from the objective world and from consciousness itself. When a sense organ, such as the eye, comes into contact with a clay pot, the reflection of the object is transmitted to the *buddhi* and, because the *buddhi* is transparent and luminous (being almost entirely *sattva*), it displays the reflection of the object (Chakrabarti 1999: 179). Certain types of sensory focus in meditation[15] help to steady the mind and lead to the acquisition of *buddhi* so that '*buddhisattva* is resplendent (*bhāsvara*) like the sky (*ākāśa*)' (PYŚ 1.36). This process is objective cognition (*saṃprajñāta samādhi*). But reflection also comes from another direction, *puruṣa*, and when the reflection of consciousness alights on *buddhi*, there is a conscious or witnessing presence, or non-objective cognition (*asaṃprajñāta samādhi*). Through the prescribed methods of rational reflection and meditation, these processes of cognition become ever more subtle and rarefied until the *buddhi* is able to cognize itself for what it is, an object, i.e. material mentality. That very cognition produces liberating knowledge of the true nature of self as consciousness, and not mind.

In Patañjali's system, there is an inextricable relation between the individuated *puruṣa* and its *buddhi*. Each separate consciousness (*pratyak-cetana*) is linked or conjoined (*saṃyoga*) to its own mind (*svabuddhi*) (PYŚ 2.23). The relation endures for an eternal period (and in the ancient world, eternity often simply indicated an unimaginably long period of time) (Chakrabarti 1999: 184). This relation endures through repeated incarnations until such time as liberation is attained.

PYŚ 1.2 informs us that, in ordinary mental states, *citta* (=*buddhi*) is pervaded by the three qualities (*guṇa*s) of clarity/balance (*sattva*), dynamism (*rajas*) and inertia (*tamas*):[16]

> Indeed the form of *sattva*, i.e. mental *sattva*, when mixed with *rajas* and *tamas* becomes attached to objects (referents) and power.
>
> (PYŚ 1.2)

Hence *buddhi* in its intermingled state (of the qualities) is very much enmeshed in worldly attachments and ambitions. However, in its ideal and natural state, *buddhi* consists only of *sattva*, which is by its very nature. There are intermediate stages towards this pure *sattva*, such as when *tamas* has been eliminated and only traces of *rajas* are left, intermingled with *sattva*:

> And precisely this [*sattva*], when the concealing of delusion is destroyed, conduces towards *dharma*, knowledge, detachment, and strength, shedding forth its light everywhere, pierced only by *rajas*.
>
> (PYŚ 1.2)

When *sattva* is pure, then *buddhi* is able to distinguish between itself (as *sattva*) and *puruṣa*. And this state of discriminating discernment (*vivekakhyāti*) is itself the liberating insight that frees one to re-identify as pure consciousness (*puruṣa*). Residing in *puruṣa* is also referred to as *citiśakti* (the power of consciousness), which 'does not transform, has no intermixture, is pure when objects are shown to it, and is eternal' (PYŚ 1.2). Consciousness is the witness of *buddhi*, and the two are said to be not alike, but also not un-alike (PYŚ 2.20). It is because of this possibility of resemblance (*buddhi* in its pure state of *sattva* is also luminous) that the existential confusion and misperception occurs. What is determined, however, is that (when associated) consciousness always knows the contents of *buddhi*; this conscious process is never interrupted (PYŚ 2.20), no matter the confusion that may reign in *buddhi*.

There are also special modes of illuminated awareness with different names such as *jyotiṣmatī* (1.36) or *prātibha* (3.33), indicating a burst or flash of understanding. These higher modes are still associated with *buddhi*, but are tending towards the self-consciousness of *puruṣa*. Indeed, the text does not shy away from the question of how the knower can be known (PYŚ 3.35) – clarifying that *buddhi-sattva* can only generate *a conception of* consciousness. Hence consciousness itself cannot be known by *buddhi*; it can only be known by *puruṣa*, i.e. through self-consciousness. However, in *pāda* 4 as the discussion develops into a refutation of the Buddhists, consciousness is also said to be knowable by another consciousness, since consciousness is individuated. So, a *puruṣa* can know itself and it can also know something of another *puruṣa*.

Egoity and mundane thought (*ahaṃkāra* and *manas*)

Ahaṃkāra (egoity) and *manas* (mundane mind) are not discussed in great depth in the text, but they are located in the evolutionary theory of the material mind. Hence the mind is sketched using a tripartite model of *buddhi*, as the most advanced and subtle mental dimension, and *manas* as belonging to the least subtle, the *liṅga* or marked (differentiated) realm of *prakṛti* (i.e. the manifest) (PYŚ 2.19).

Egoity or the feeling of 'I am' (*asmitā*) is associated with the senses. Indeed, the senses are said to be particular features of egoity and only by focusing on egoity itself can one gain control or mastery of the senses (PYŚ 3.47). (See also the discussion of *asmitā* in 'Chapter 3: Ontology'.) In this meditative identity (*saṃyama*), egoity is placed in a sequence of five stages. To conquer the senses (*indriyajayaḥ*), one must in turn meditate (1) on perception itself (*grahaṇa*) with its universal and particular aspects, (2) on the essential nature of a substance, (3) on one's own 'I-am-ness', (4) on the material qualities (the three *guṇas*) and (5) on the impelling drive or purpose of the *guṇa*s. In this act of increasingly subtle understanding of the nature of reality, the egoic 'I' is merely an object in a sequence of objects to be properly known.

Manas is grouped with the five elements in a 5+1 model: earth, water, fire, air, space and mind (*manas*), where it marks a transition point between subtle and gross materiality. Whereas the workings of the mundane mind are directly observable and are part of the gross world, *manas* also orients inwards to lead to the ego, which is a subtle phenomenon, superseded only in the mental realm by *buddhi*, the principle of intelligence or awareness (PYŚ 2.19).

Mind as seedbed

Another key model of mind, heavily indebted to Buddhist thought, is an ontological metaphor of the mind as a field of botanical growth. This field (*kṣetra*) has an invisible substratum (*āśraya*) which is, in effect, a seedbed for all kinds of psychological seeds of future dispositions – good and bad. Awareness is the tending of the soil and it exercises control by weeding out bad or undesirable seeds of growth, while cultivating other seeds to full fruit. Here, the exercising of control refers to the many techniques of reflection and meditation that are offered in the *Pātañjalayogaśāstra*. The seeds of afflictions (discussed above) are particularly dangerous to the mental field and must be scorched to prevent any future germination. This can be accomplished by certain techniques such as enumerative reflection (*prasaṃkhyāna*), which is the exercise of cognitive disjunction from particular objects in meditation (O'Brien-Kop 2018). Ultimately, however, all cognitive techniques lead to non-cognitive modes of knowing (such as the level of concentration called 'cloud of *dharma*'):

> **The concentration of the cloud of dharma[17] exists for one who possesses discriminating discernment in every way and for whom there is no interest even in enumerative reflection (*prasaṃkhyāna*).** If this Brahmin is without interest even in enumerative reflection, then he does not strive whatsoever. Then, for one who is without attachment, there exists in every way discriminating discernment alone. Because of the destruction of the seed of [mental] predisposition (*saṃskāra*), interior ideations do not arise; then for him there exists the concentration that is called cloud of *dharma*.
>
> (PYŚ 4.29)

If awareness is not consistently applied (using techniques such as *prasaṃkhyāna*), however, then the seeds of negative predispositions may sprout, flourish and proliferate. Again, awareness has the opportunity to intercede and to cut such growth by branch and root (PYŚ 4.30). But if this chance is missed, the attainment of maturity by such forms in the mind contributes to one's karmic store, with seeds and their propensities carrying over into future lifetimes – delaying existential freedom yet further.

Limitations of pre-conditioned knowledge

*Saṃskāra*s are the predispositions that are reinforced (imprinted) by repeated mental activities. Indeed, the mutually reinforcing nature of predispositions and general mental processes (*vrtti*s) (such as volitions) is spelled out for us:

> Thus *saṃskāra*s are made by these very same *vṛtti*s, and *vṛtti*s are made by *saṃskāra*s. Thus the cycle of *saṃskāra*s and *vṛtti*s turns without interruption.
>
> (PYŚ 1.5)

One of the goals of this yoga philosophy is to rid the mind entirely of its predispositions through which our present knowledge and actions are preconditioned by the past. There are various techniques to eliminate these impressions, which are central to the reproductive mechanisms of *karma*. Ranganathan (2017) translates *saṃskāra*s as 'prejudices' – perhaps with a nod to Gadamer's notions of prejudice as a conditioned or prior judgement (pre-judgement). This link between *saṃskāra*s and pre-judgement is also reflected in *saṃskāra*s as the source of memory (PYŚ 1.11), since memory informs judgement. How are such unwanted predispositions to be eliminated? The primary technique is to attain the state called non-cognitive concentration in which the mental processes stop and all that remains are the specific and positive predispositions that are conducive to liberation (PYŚ 1.51). PYŚ 3.9 also makes it clear that these active predispositions are 'constituent elements of the mind (*cittadharma*)' but they are not ideation (*pratyaya*) itself. Hence, even when ideation is stopped (*cittavṛttinirodha*), the *saṃskāra*s prevail. Through the increase in moments of cessation (*nirodha*) and the tranquillized flow (*praśāntavāhitā*; PYŚ 3.10) of the mind, negative predispositions are gradually transformed into dispositions that conduce towards cessation, until finally eradication occurs. Once these predispositions have performed their function (i.e. directed the mind towards true recognition), they too cease to be, thereby signalling freedom from the cycle of karmic repercussion (PYŚ 1.18; 1.51). There will be no more actions and no more effects after this point.

The examination of the *saṃskāra*s also has a deeply psychological function in terms of understanding one's own past actions, behaviours and attitudes. This is framed metaphysically as knowledge of one's past lives (YS 3.18). Because the scrutiny of the predispositions reveals the intrinsic information of place, time, cause and experience contained therein (e.g. one cannot examine one's tendency to anger without a sense of where, when and why this emotion last took place), this is how details of past existences are thrown up into conscious light. There is no need to rationalize this statement in the terms of contemporary psychology. The text simply adheres to the theory of transmigration, and this needs to be accepted as part of the epistemic frame when we read Patañjali's text. Nonetheless, the theory of the predispositions does describe a familiar contemporary psychological process of trying to analyse why one's personality appears to be stuck on such-and-such tendencies or patterns.

In many senses, the description of how knowledge is formed is entirely restricted to the sphere of the mind, which is located in *prakrti*. Less is said about how 'pure knowing' operates in the realm of consciousness (*puruṣa*), and perhaps this realm is ineffable (an ultimate, non-cognitive knowing). And so some questions remain about the state of liberated knowledge. These include not only the central phenomenological question of how consciousness can 'know' itself, but also the more prosaic concerns about liberated knowledge: How does it feel? What does it look like? In what way can a liberated consciousness 'see' other liberated consciousnesses? Is there a kind of camaraderie of isolated liberated selves? And so forth. Without empirical reports on such states, any proposed answers remain theoretical or speculative.

Discussion questions

1. What is your evaluation of the *Yogasūtra*'s threefold model of mind: awareness, egoity and mundane operations. Can this model describe contemporary understandings of how the mind functions?
2. In your worldview, which of the six *pramāṇa*s would you include as valid bases of knowledge? Are there other forms of knowing not included here that you consider important?
3. In today's information-rich world, how do we judge what is 'correct perception' or 'right knowledge'?

Further reading

Bilimoria, P. (2018) 'Pramāṇa Epistemology: Origins and Developments' in Bilimoria, P. (ed.) *History of Indian Philosophy*. Routledge History of World Philosophies. London and New York: Routledge.

Chakrabarti, K. (1999) 'The Sāṃkhya View and the Nyāya Critique' in *Classical Indian Philosophy of Mind: The Nyāya Dualist Tradition*. Delhi: Motilal Banarsidass.

Chakravarthi, R. (2007) 'Chapter 2: Consciousness and Luminosity: On How Knowledge Is Possible' in *Indian Philosophy and the Consequences of Knowledge: Themes in Ethics, Metaphysics and Soteriology*. Oxford and New York: Ashgate Publishing.

Chapple, C. (2012) '*Siddhi*s in the *Yogasūtra*' in Jacobsen, K. A. (ed.) *Yoga Powers: Extraordinary Capacities Attained through Meditation and Concentration*. Leiden: Brill, 223–40.

Cousins, L. (1992) '*Vitakka/vitarka* and *Vicāra*: Stages of *Samādhi* in Buddhism and Yoga' in *Indo-Iranian Journal* 35.2/3: 137–57.

Dunne, J. (2007) 'Realizing the Unreal: Dharmakīrti's Theory of Yogic Perception' in *Journal of Indian Philosophy*, 34.5: 497–519.

Endo, K. (2000) '*Prasaṃkhyāna* in the *Yogabhāṣya*' in Mayeda, S. (ed.) *The Way to Liberation: Indological Studies in Japan*. New Delhi: Manohar (Japanese Studies on South Asia, 3).

Macdonald, A. (2009) 'Knowing Nothing: Candrakīrti and Yogic Perception' in Franco, Eli (eds.) *Yogic Perception, Meditation and Altered States of Consciousness*. Vienna: Verlag der Österreichischen Akademie der Wissenschaften, 133–68.

Philips, S. (2019) 'Classical Indian Epistemology' Stanford Encyclopedia of Philosophy (on-line publication, entry revised March 2019). http://plato.stanford.edu/entries/epistemology-india/.

Raveh, D. (2012) 'Rethinking *Prajñā*: *Yogasūtra* 1.49 under a Philosophical Magnifying Glass' in *Exploring the Yogasūtra: Philosophy and Translation*. London and New York: Continuum.

5

Logic: The thread of reasoning

Chapter outline

Because of the immediate and obvious relevance of its concepts of 'practice' to our contemporary world, the character of the *Yogasūtra* as a work of formal philosophy is sometimes overlooked. Yet logic is a key means in Indian philosophy, used to correct wrong views and to know reality as it is – and hence to become liberated. The very format of the text as a *sūtra* indicates its conventional philosophical purpose with some measure of logic. Not only are *sūtra*s condensed doctrines or discourses with mnemonic value (i.e. designed to be memorized), but they are also, as the word *sūtra* (lit. thread) itself indicates, 'beads' of thought that are threaded in a specific pattern that is underpinned by logic, reasoning and argumentation. A *sūtra* text was designed systematically in order to be digested systematically. Hence the text opens like many other philosophical texts by stating its subject (*viṣaya*), its scope or context (*saṃbandha*) and the goal (*prayojana*).

Beads on a thread: How to construct an argument

The opening two *sūtra*s announce the text's status as a *śāstra* on yoga followed by a definition of what yoga is – this outlines the formal subject (*viṣaya*) of the text:

> *atha yoga anuśāsanam*
> ***yogaś cittavṛttinirodhaḥ*** (YS 1.2).
> Now the exposition on yoga.
> **Yoga is the cessation of mental processes.**

The means to achieve yoga is introduced at YS 1.12 as practice (*abhyāsa*) and dispassion (*vairāgya*) – and this indicates the scope (*saṃbandha*) of the text, i.e. this is what the treatise will be discussing. The goal is not defined with a general term for liberation such as *mokṣa*, but rather with the more technical terms *samādhi* (concentration) and *kaivalya* (isolation, separation). We see then the fulfilment (between *sūtra* 1.1 and *sūtra* 1.12) of the opening intent of the *Yogasūtra*: to establish the parameters of its topic, a technique called 'yoga'. The structure of this opening is concordant with the other orthodox (*āstika*) *sūtra* texts.[1]

The text then proceeds according to an organizing principle, as follows: (a) a proposition is asserted, (b) a series of sub-points may be stated to add further detail, to justify, to clarify or, indeed, to reach a sub-conclusion and then (c) a new proposition is asserted. Thus, thematic sub-sections exist within the text, and each proposition follows on logically from the prior statements in a reasoned sequence. The *sūtra*s are ordered so as to present main assertions that are subdivided into supporting or explanatory points. We can see this pattern unfolding in YS 1.4–1.11, in which the mental modifications (*vṛtti*s) are introduced, enumerated and each qualified in further detail.

Chapter on concentration[2]

1.1 Now the exposition on yoga.

1.2 Yoga is the cessation of mental processes.

1.3 Then the seer abides in their own form.

1.4 Otherwise, there is the condition of possessing the form of the modifications.

1.5 The modifications are fivefold – defiled and undefiled:

1.6 Valid bases of knowledge, erroneous cognition, mental construction, sleep, memory.

1.7 The valid bases of knowledge are: perception, inference, testimony.

1.8 Erroneous cognition is false knowledge, not of a correct form.

1.9 Mental construction without a real object results from verbal cognition.

1.10 Sleep is a mental process which has as its support the awareness of the absence [of the other mental processes].

1.11 Memory is not letting go of objects that have been experienced.

1.12 They [i.e. the modifications] are ceased by practice and dispassion.

1.13 In that state of cessation when there is constancy, effort becomes practice.

1.14 But it [practice] takes a long time of exercising care without interruption to be firmly grounded.

1.15 Dispassion is the technical term for mastery in one who is without thirst for the object, whether seen or revealed.

1.16 The highest [dispassion] is from the discernment of *puruṣa*, having no thirst for the qualities (*guṇas*).

The five mental operations (*vṛttis*) are introduced at 1.5. Then each of the five is in turn defined. For example, YS 1.6 introduces valid bases of knowledge (*pramāṇas*) as one of the operations and in the next *sūtra* (1.7) further explains *pramāṇa* as perception, inference and reliable testimony (*pratyakṣa, anumāna, āgama*). (See 'Chapter 4: Epistemology'.) The *sūtra* does not linger further on the *pramāṇas*, but turns immediately in YS 1.8 to the next mental operation, erroneous cognition (*viparyaya*), which is explained with just one statement:

> **Erroneous cognition is false knowledge, not of a correct form.**
>
> (YS 1.8)[3]

The sub-section list ends when 1.12 zooms back out to a new point, about practice and dispassion. Hence, understanding of Patañjali's text is enhanced by reading the *sūtras* in order from start to finish.

However, within the *Yogasūtra*, intricate patterns of logical connection are also woven back and forth between the *sūtras* and the commentary (*bhāṣya*). For example, after a long excursus into the nature of *īśvara*, different methods of objective concentration, and the nine impediments to the yogic method, the commentary rounds up a discussion on the distractions (impediments) that were listed at PYŚ 1.31 by stating:

> These are the distractions, the obstacles to *samādhi*, which are to be ceased by that same practice and dispassion. There, in concluding the subject (*viṣaya*) of practice, he says:
>
> **For the sake of warding off, practice on one principle.**
>
> **(YS 1.32)**

Here, *sūtra* 1.32 links back to YS 1.12, which introduced dispassion and practice. Since YS 1.12, we have been led through the constituent features of practice and dispassion in order, and this concluding section on practice now demonstrates how certain impediments inhibit successful practice and offers solutions ('warding off') on how to dispel such obstacles. It is all neatly worked out and signposted, and these reasoned structures aid the reader, or listener, to keep their place in a complex and unfolding bundle of instructions.

Let's consider another example, *sūtra* 2.16, which also helps us to trace the logical flow of the *sūtras*:

> **Suffering that is yet to occur can be stopped.**
>
> (YS 2.16)[4]

This *sūtra* can be read as a standalone statement (as aphorisms often are), but since it forms part of a longer sub-section of discourse, our understanding is enhanced if we read it in context. This means that we have to work backwards from this *sūtra* to pick up the thread of the reasoning: this *sūtra* on suffering is part of a statement on the theory of *karma* in relation to the afflictions (*kleśas*), and the afflictions, in turn, form a sub-section in the opening exposition on the active method (*kriyā yoga*) at the start of the second *pāda* (chapter):

Chapter on practice[5]

2.1 The yoga of action (*kriyā yoga*) is austerity, recitation and contemplation on *īśvara*.

2.2 It (*kriyā yoga*) has the purpose of cultivating concentration and of causing the reduction of the afflictions (*kleśas*).

2.3 The afflictions are nescience, egoity, attachment, aversion and clinging to life.

2.4 Nescience is the field of the others [i.e. the afflictions], be they dormant, attenuated, interrupted or manifest.

2.5 Nescience is [mistaking] impermanence, impurity, suffering, and non-self for permanence, purity, happiness and perception of self.

2.6 Egoity is [viewing] the power of the seer (*dṛś*) and of the seen (*darśana*) as one entity alone.

2.7 Attachment follows happiness.

2.8 Aversion follows suffering.

2.9 Clinging to life is in the flow of one's nature, even for the wise.

2.10 The subtle [afflictions] are to be quitted by involution (*pratiprasava*).

2.11 Regarding those modifications (*vṛttis*), to be quitted by [meditative] absorption (*dhyāna*):

2.12 The karmic substratum [*āśaya*] has affliction as its root [and] is to be experienced in the present birth as well as future ones.

2.13 When the root [of affliction] exists, its retribution is birth, lifespan and experience.

2.14 Due to the cause of merit or demerit, they [birth, lifespan, experience] have fruits of joy or sorrow.

> **2.15 For the discriminating one, all is suffering alone, due to the struggle of the modified *guṇa*s and by means of the suffering [produced by] change, pain and predispositions (*saṃskāra*s).**
> **2.16 Suffering that is yet to occur can be stopped.**
> **2.17 The cause of what is to be abandoned [stopped] is the [mistaken] conjunction of the seer and the seen.**

So, the logical order and arrangement of *sūtra*s in the above section (YS 2.1–2.17) proceeds thus to build an overall argument, which I have further condensed, paraphrased and summarized here for clarity:

> *Kriyā yoga* has three components, which stop the mind and reduce the five afflictions.
> Mental involution stops the subtle afflictions.
> Meditation stops the mind.
> But there are some persistent afflictions rooted in the mind that affect *karma*.
> *Karma* can be good and bad, but for the yogin it is all bad (suffering).
> However, **future suffering (produced by *karma*) – can be stopped,** if one can stop the false mixing up of consciousness and materiality.

I have highlighted in bold the statement that reflects *sūtra* 2.16. We can see that by reading this *sūtra* (or any *sūtra*) in context (in the flow), our understanding of its meaning and import is deepened. The thread of the reasoned sections of discourse is often submerged in the detail of the commentary, but with careful reading one can identify it and bring it to the surface.

One further example is the introduction of the fourfold medical paradigm at PYŚ 2.15 to explain bondage and liberation (the disease, the cause, the remedy, the means – also discussed below in relation to the Four Noble Truths).[6] These four stages of spiritual formation are still being discussed when the commentary to YS 2.24 ends. It reminds us where we are in the discussion by stating that it has so far covered the first two of these (the disease and the cause) and will now discuss the remedy or outcome of liberation, which it does in 2.24 before moving on to the fourth component at 2.25, the means to liberation (identified as discriminating discernment, which produces sevenfold knowledge) (PYŚ 2.26–27) (see Table 2 in Chapter 3: Ontology'). The text then moves on to another means, the eightfold model of practice or *aṣṭāṅga yoga* (PYŚ 2.28 onwards). An integrated reading of the *sūtra* and commentary helps us to fully understand where *aṣṭāṅga yoga* sits in the overall discourse. *Aṣṭāṅga yoga* is one of the methods appropriate for those engaged and involved in the world with active minds. It is an instance of the means to liberation as outlined in the fourfold medical-style diagnosis of the existential problem – which is introduced at YS 2.15 and starts to wind up at 2.27 (wherein the fourfold model is re-located in a larger model of seven stages) as the exposition of *aṣṭāṅga* is begun. The commentarial lead-in to *sūtra* 2.28 states:

> the means to escape (*hānopāya*) is the perfection of discriminating discernment (*vivekakhyāti*), and only practice can ensure success. Hence this section is begun.
>
> (PYŚ 2.28)

And so the discussion of the eight auxiliaries opens – as part of the expansion and explanation of what constitutes 'the means to escape' in the fourfold paradigm of disease-cause-remedy-means. Although the eightfold method has often been extracted and read independently, I argue that being able to see how this section on *aṣṭāṅga yoga* fits in to the overall logical structure of the *Yogasūtra* enhances our understanding of its significance considerably.[7]

Inference

We can by now appreciate the value of reading Patañjali's text as a sustained act of reasoning. The whole of the *Yogasūtra* is structured in this way, with the beads of truth threaded to create a system. The text as a whole develops discursively according to principles of logical coherence, i.e. as we read, we can identify arguments in which propositions are arranged so as to provide support for the truth of a conclusion. It is vital to recall that inference is one of the three valid bases of knowledge, indicating that this whole system of yoga philosophy rests on logic as well as direct perception and authority. A definition of inference is laid out at PYŚ 1.7:

> Inference (*anumāna*) is that mental process (*vṛtti*) whose principal object is the determination of the universal and which includes the relation of the same kind of class as the inferred (object) and excludes the class of difference (*bhinna*).
>
> (PYŚ 1.7)

Patañjali employs the well-established rules of logicians to reason the truth of the yoga system and relies on inference as a way to establish universal truths.

If knowledge via perception could not be secured, then Sāṃkhya and Yoga agreed that inference (*anumāna*) was an acceptable alternative. The process of flawless reasoning was developed in the school of Nyāya from around the first century BCE,[8] and the word *anumāna* indicates 'after' knowledge – i.e. the conclusion that follows a process of reasoning. The process of inference was to move from a conceptual sign or mark (*liṅga*), through reasons (*hetu*) to a certain conclusion (*sādhya* or *siddhānta*). This was often conducted via the process of syllogistic reasoning, which, unlike the western Aristotelian three-step syllogism, moved through five stages (*avayava*) that incorporated a principle of invariable concomitance (*vyāpti*) between two events (such as: where there is smoke, there is always fire). What is key in Indian arguments or proofs is that the philosophers are not just reasoning for the sake of validity, but also for the sake of truth (true knowledge). In Indian logic, if an argument is valid, it is true and vice versa. This is distinct from western logic in which truth and validity were often decoupled. In Aristotelian logic, it is sufficient in a syllogistic argument to be concerned with a hypothetical relationship between true propositions – such that if the premises are true and in a certain relationship then the conclusion cannot be false, but also if the premises are not true and are in a certain relationship then the conclusion may be valid but not true. Indian logic, however, deals not only with the relationships between propositions, but also states the truth or falsity of objects in the world as part of the same and valid process. Hence the product of reasoning (conclusion) is linked to the process of reasoning (valid argument) and cannot be decoupled.

Debate and argumentation

At the time of the coalescing and final redaction of the *Pātañjalayogaśāstra* (*c.* second to fifth centuries CE), the shared culture of debate ensured an intellectual milieu in which interaction between different schools of thought often took place explicitly through refutation.[9]

We cannot underestimate the significance of the role of debate in the transmission of ideas between schools of thought in this period. As Gombrich reminds us, the Buddha's teachings began in an atmosphere of debate in which the Buddha was necessarily winning over converts from Brahmanism using the 'skilful means' of argument (Gombrich 1996: 1–26). In this respect, debate was not only built in to Buddhism but to all schools of this time. In the early centuries of the first millennium CE, there was also the broader formal context of philosophical debates at the royal courts (Bronkhorst 2006: 303). The stakes of philosophical debates were sometimes high, with material consequences such as punishments, beatings and even death (Anacker 1984: 20). Although such debates were initially organized at court where participants from different schools were obliged by the king to engage with each other institutionally, these encounters became embedded in the scholarly culture, so that it became commonplace to critically refine one's own position by engaging with those of opponents (Bronkhorst 2006: 303).

If oral debate was an inherent part of intellectual life in the first centuries of the CE, it also filtered into the literary apparatus of the written tradition, albeit less dynamically. Studies of intertextuality have demonstrated that there are linked passages and arguments between the *Pātañalayogaśāstra* and several Buddhist treatises of the period, suggesting that they were all forged in an atmosphere of debate (Maas 2020; O'Brien-Kop 2021). For example, the voluminous Buddhist Sarvāstivāda *Mahāvibhāṣā*, which forms one basis for Vasubandhu's *Abhidharmakośabhāṣya*, is itself a systematic record of the debates that occurred in a conference called by the Emperor Kaniṣka in *c.* first to second century CE (Anacker 1984: 12). Those whose views are quoted include the Buddhist philosophers Dharmatrāta, Ghoṣaka, Vasumitra and Buddhadeva. Anacker notes: '[t]his tremendous work often reads like a committee report, with widely varying opinions being offered' (Anacker 1984: 12). The *Mahāvibhāṣā* shows acquaintance with Vaiśeṣika and Sāṃkhya (Bronkhorst 2006: 290).[10] Vasubandhu refutes both the Sāṃkhyas and the Nyāya-Vaiśeṣikas in the *Abhidharmakośabhāṣya*[11] and he refutes the Sāṃkhyas in his *Paramārthasaptati*.[12] The *Sāṃkhyakārikā* closes by claiming that it is a distillation of the key points of the *Ṣaṣṭitantra* (a prior but lost Sāṃkhya work) without a consideration of opponents' views (SK 72), indicating that such views were originally laid out in the *Ṣaṣṭitantra*. Indeed, the Brahmanical *sūtra* format, as Tubb and Boose remind us, is essentially a remnant from oral presentation structured via logical argumentation, a 'series of signposts in an oral argument' (Tubb and Boose 2007: 1). In short, argumentative pluralism was built in to the philosophical texts of the early first millennium CE in India and as Pollock states: 'The classicity of Indian philosophy lies precisely in the development of reasoned argument in the face of wholesale conceptual assaults' (Pollock 2015). The *Pātañjalayogaśāstra* was produced within and against this backdrop of formal debate.

The degree to which intellectual identities, such as philosophical standpoints, were strictly tied to religious identities is not clear. Nicholson has argued that the traditional divisions between *āstika* and *nāstika* schools are better framed doctrinally as 'affirmer' and 'denier' rather than 'orthodox' and 'heterodox' (Nicholson 2010: 176–9). In his view, such school divisions showcase a medieval doxographic perspective that did not necessarily reflect complex and self-perceived doctrinal identities in the earlier periods. Although scholars retrospectively label the classical logicians as 'Buddhist logicians' or 'Nyāya logicians', for example, those figures may have understood themselves to be simply 'logicians'. Similarly, if we regard yoga as a philosophical training, then perhaps a yoga philosopher was first a foremost a philosopher, and not essentially a 'Brahmin' or 'Buddhist' philosopher.[13]

The interwoven nature of Brahmin and Buddhist rationalities in the early common era has been well depicted. In order to understand the formal philosophical context of the *Yogasūtra*, therefore, one needs to read beyond Sāṃkhya into the other *āstika* schools and, further, into Buddhist and Jain texts. For example, Sāṃkhya and Buddhist Sarvāstivāda Abhidharma share structural tendencies towards systematic enumeration in their ontologies (Larson 1989).[14] Pātañjala Yoga and Buddhist Yogācāra share inferential propositions in their solutions to get rid of the mental states called afflictions (O'Brien-Kop 2021: 95–112). Larson (1989) postulates that the *Yogasūtra* and its first commentary emerged from a dialogue between the Sāṃkhya thinker Vindhyavāsin and the Buddhist Vasubandhu. For Larson, it was Vindhyavāsin who was responsible for the radical philosophical hybridity of the *Pātañjalayogaśāstra* and not Patañjali, who was merely a textual compiler in the shadows.[15] We cannot, of course, verify such claims, but it is important to recognize that the *Yogasūtra* was not produced in an intellectual vacuum, but was a response to the main philosophical and religious debates of its time in South Asia.

Refutation and polyphony

Śāstric texts (treatises) are a distilled product of oral debates that occurred between philosophers of different stripes, and hence there is a pan-Indian tradition that transcends individual schools such as Nyāya, Vedānta, Yoga or Buddhism. This is reflected in the shared terminology and techniques of argumentation between many treatises, regardless of affiliation. Within the treatises themselves, we can find evidence of such debates (a) in traces of the dialogic exchanges of debate, (b) in direct refutations of rival philosophical positions and (c) in more subtle layers of conceptual interaction.

The traces of live debate are embedded in the structure of argumentation found in a śāstric text, which is polyphonic. This means that several voices and viewpoints are employed to develop a logical argument. There are a number of ways in which this polyphony is achieved. One is to simply declare an intention to set out a number of distinct views. One noteworthy example of this practice occurs at PYŚ 2.23 in which some nine possible answers are listed in response to the question 'what is this "non-seeing"'?[16] (See also 'Chapter 4: Epistemology'.) After the differing viewpoints have been briefly described, the statement is made: 'These then are the different views (*vikalpa*) derived from the *śāstras*'.[17] Another approach to polyphony is to include a potted or distilled version of a live oral debate in which a question is posed and answered, e.g. PYŚ 2.13 on the question of whether a single action causes just one future incarnation or multiple incarnations (see O'Brien-Kop forthcoming). The typical structure is that the author first puts forward the view of an opponent (*pūrvapakṣin*) and then proceeds to demolish that view. This word *pūrvapakṣin* means 'the earlier proponent' and indicates that although introduced early on in an exposition, the *pūrvapakṣin*'s position is then left behind. This refutation often entails not just a rejection of the content of the *pūrvapakṣin*'s assertions, but also the epistemology, i.e. the *pramāṇa*s or valid bases of those knowledge claims. After developing an argument, the author then arrives at the *siddhānta*, the conclusion or proof. This technique may be summed up in the following way:

1. state the opponent's view: the *pūrvapakṣa*
2. refute that view: the *khaṇḍana*
3. advance one's own conclusion: the *siddhānta*

Hence any philosophical system not only states its own position on a range of doctrines, but includes a *précis* and summary of the rival's position and objections. Hence such systems may be termed dialectical.

Sometimes the refutations are formal expositions that are part of the *sūtra*s (see the discussion of *cittamātra* below), but in other instances the refutations are more subtly embedded in the commentary. One example of this follows *sūtra* 1.32, which concludes the section on practice (*abhyāsa*) by explaining that the obstacles to yoga can be prevented by focus on one principle or object. However, the next line introduces an objection or contrary point of view, recognizably that of a (straw man) Buddhist:

> But for one [who says that] the mind is always on one object, [since its] focus is only momentary, the mind is always only one-pointed and there is no distraction.
>
> (PYŚ 1.32)

This Buddhist position on the nature of mind (as an awareness that is momentary and hence only ever singular in its fleeting focus) is then refuted with a challenge from Patañjali, who asserts that one-pointed focus actually requires deliberate effort:

> But [only] when [the mind] is withdrawn from all directions onto the object of concentration, does it become one-pointed – therefore it is not always [already] focused on one object.
>
> (PYŚ 1.32)

The next sentence introduces another typical Buddhist objection, and so the back and forth continues throughout the rest of the commentary on 1.32 until a sub-conclusion is reached by Patañjali: 'Therefore the mind is stable, has multiple objects (*anekārtham*), and is singular.' In each of these points, the theory of mind is a refutation of Buddhist doctrine: hence the mind is stable (not in flux nor momentary), the mind holds multiple objects and ideas at once (not one at time as in the theory of momentariness) and the mind is singular or unitary (not a collocation of similar and dissimilar ideas experienced discretely).

The dialogue of debate in also evident in the extended commentary to *Yogasūtra* 3.13–3.15, in which there is a defence of the Yoga-Sāṃkhya conception of time and a critical assault on the Buddhist Sarvāstivāda theory of the 'three time periods' as co-existing at once (Maas 2020). Leaving aside the content of the argument for now (discussed in

'Chapter 2: Metaphysics'), the discursive and syntactic style reproduces the oration of formal debate. In this case, the 'others' are, once again, the Buddhists:

> [Objection] An objector states ... (*apara āha* ...)
> [Answer] This, however, is not a fallacy (fault), since ... (*ayam adoṣaḥ. kasmāt* ...).
>
> (PYŚ 3.13)

And:

> Certain persons have claimed ... (*kaiścid uktaḥ* ...)
> However, there is no fault in it (our position), since ... (*nāsau doṣaḥ. kasmāt* ...).
>
> (PYŚ 3.13)

Let us now review some specific instances in which the chief opponents of Patañjali's system, the Buddhists, are refuted explicitly and at length.

Refutation of Buddhist idealism

The fourth chapter of the *Pātañjalayogaśāstra* contains a polemic against a Mahāyāna doctrine referred to as *cittamātra*, or mind-only (idealism). The *sūtra*s and commentary from PYŚ 4.14–23[18] address the relationship between mind (*citta*) and the external object, entailing a refutation of the Buddhist position.[19] Patañjali concludes that those who believe that this world is mind-only are pitiable in their delusion.[20]

The commentary to *Yogasūtra* 4.23 leaves little doubt that it is a specific critique of the Buddhist Yogācāra school or doctrine – and most likely refers to the works of Vasubandhu or Asaṅga. The Yogācāra epistemology was known by different names: not only *cittamātratā* ([the doctrine that] there is nothing but mind) but also *vijñānavāda* (consciousness doctrine) and *vijñaptimatratā* ([the doctrine that] there is nothing but representation). The first exposition of the doctrine of mind-only or representation-only is commonly traced to Vasubandhu's works.[21] However, Asaṅga also uses the term *cittamātra* in association with the theory of eight consciousnesses set forth in the *Yogācārabhūmiśāstra*, as well as in his other works.[22] Notably, Burley does not agree that Patañjali's *sūtras* on the mind-only doctrine are engaged with Buddhist ideas. Rather, Burley argues that this section of the fourth *pāda* 'exhibits no signs of being directed against Yogācāra or any other form of Buddhism' (Burley 2007: 82). Burley posits that this attribution of anti-Yogācāra polemicism is merely a mistaken view of the subsequent commentators perpetuated over time, and that the passage is entirely concordant with the internal 'non-realist' position of the *Yogasūtra* itself. However, given the specificity of *cittamātra* as a label associated with the Buddhist Yogācāra School and that Patañjali's system constructs a broadly realist worldview, it seems that Patañjali's polemic is directed at this stream of Buddhism specifically.

Refutation of the Four Noble Truths and the Middle Way

Although Pātañjala yoga is understood to be largely derived from or at least concordant with the Sāṃkhya system, Sāṃkhya itself is rarely discussed explicitly in the *Pātañjalayogaśāstra*. Indeed, the foundational Sāṃkhya philosopher Vārṣagaṇya is directly cited only once in the *Pātañjalayogaśāstra*, in relation to ontological matters (PYŚ 3.53). However, the Sāṃkhya doctrine of *satkāryavāda* (the effect pre-exists in the cause) is referenced indirectly in the commentary to YS 2.15 in a discussion of self.

> Of these, *saṃsāra*, because it contains great suffering, is to be escaped. The cause of that which is to be escaped (i.e. suffering) is the conjunction of *pradhāna* (unmanifest *prakṛti*) with *puruṣa*. Escape (*hānam*) is when there is absolute cessation of the conjunction. The means of escaping is correct seeing. [In correct seeing] the intrinsic nature of the one who escapes is not something that should be accepted or rejected: if it is rejected, the consequence is the doctrine of its annihilation, and if accepted (*upādāne*) the doctrine that it has a

> cause. When both [doctrines] are denied, the doctrine that it is eternal [follows]; this is correct seeing.
>
> (PYŚ 2.15)[23]

This passage argues that self is an eternal given and is not something that is 'caused' – which is in line with Sāṃkhya ontology. However, the passage also functions as a refutation of the views that the self can be annihilated or caused. The broader context of the passage is a refashioning of the Four Noble Truths of Buddhism (suffering, the cause of suffering, cessation, the path), so that the Buddhist paradigm is co-opted and filled with Sāṃkhya doctrinal content. But additionally Patañjali is creating a dialogic response to the Buddha's rejection of two 'extreme' views: the doctrine of annihilation (*ucchedavāda*) and the doctrine of an eternal self (*śaśvatavāda*).[24] Thus Patañjali appropriates the Buddha's critique of the two extremes and uses it to bolster the Sāṃkhya-Yoga position on the self: if the true self is not caused and does not perish, then it must be eternal. Often, schools did not have to be explicitly named in textual refutation; it was enough to refer to their doctrines alone.

The nature of philosophical debate in the early period means that we cannot regard the *Pātañjalayogaśāstra* as anything less than intertextual. If philosophical authors were not referring to each others' work via processes of refutation and co-option, they would have been going against the intellectual grain. Such sparring dialogues only partially reflect the need to distinguish one's position on the basis of difference. Rather, debates were used to explore the weaknesses in one's own argument in order to strengthen it for the next round. It seems likely that schools such as Sāṃkhya, Yoga and Sarvāstivāda Abhidharma co-evolved in a milieu of debate, and this is certainly reflected in these schools' emphases on ontological categorization (putting things in boxes). Reasoned debate, then, was an environment in which difference cloaked similarity; on the surface these schools refuted each other, but in the detail of the debate they co-constructed their own concepts in partnership with their opponents.

Discussion questions

1. What are the advantages of using inference to demonstrate truth, rather than sense perception or an appeal to authority?
2. Early Indian philosophical systems were devised in a relation of debate with other schools. Does this still happen today?
3. If you have read the *Yogasūtra* (in translation), can you summarize its overall argument in a three-stage or five-stage syllogism (supporting and linked premises followed by a conclusion)?

Further reading

Copi, I. et al. (2011) Chapter 13: 'Introduction to Indian Logic: Nyaya, Bauddha, and Jaina' in Copi, I. et al. (eds.) *Introduction to Logic*, 14th edition. International (India): Pearson Education.

Ganeri, J. (2001) *Philosophy in Classical India: The Proper Work of Reason*. London: Routledge.

Gupta, B. (2009) *Reason and Experience in Indian Philosophy*. Delhi: Indian Council of Philosophical Research.

Matilal, B. K. S. (1999) *The Character of Logic in India*, ed. Ganeri and Tiwari. New York: SUNY.

Matilal, B. K. S. (1985) *Logic, Language and Reality*. Delhi: Motilal Banarsidass.

Raghuramaraju, A. (2007) *Debates in Indian Philosophy: Classical, Colonial, and Contemporary*. Oxford: Oxford University Press.

6

Philosophy of language

Chapter outline

Given that the name of the author-editor of the *Yogasūtra* is most likely a tribute to the authority (and lineage) of the renowned grammarian Patañjali (*c.* second century BCE), it would be remiss to overlook the role of philosophy of language in this text. Some scholars even posit that parts of the *Yogasūtra* correlate to – or pay homage to – the ground-breaking work of the earlier grammar treatises, among the first works in which the conventions of *śāstra* and *sūtra* were established. At the very least, in order to understand practical techniques (*kriyā yoga*) that entail recitation of key statements of truth (from the Vedas), the reader benefits from a grounding in the relationship between sound and language in Indian philosophy and the archaic relationship between language and reality, understood as a form of direct referentialism. The relation of object, word-referent and word-sound in Indian philosophy is well worth investigating and is more connected to contemporary Western philosophy of language that might be assumed; after all, the European founder of linguistics, Ferdinand de Saussure, was a scholar of Sanskrit grammar.

There are several contexts in which language is discussed reflexively by Patañjali. Some of the more obvious contexts include the well known acceptance of the authority of Vedic language, the effects of scriptural utterance (recitation) and cosmogonic understandings of a primordial syllable (*akṣara*) that gives rise to the world. However, language is also analysed in more technical contexts of grammar and epistemology. What are the rules of a system of linguistic utterance, such that meaning can be grasped? How does language direct us to the truth or obscure it? What is the relationship between a word and the object it denotes? As a learned treatise of philosophy, addressing such questions was an expected feature of Patañjali's *sūtra* text in the early Common Era.

A brief consideration of some of the positions of the various schools on language is helpful in this regard. Indian philosophy of language is also bound up with a metaphysical understanding of Sanskrit, understood to be unique and perfect[1] as a language system, as well as divinely revealed. The first treatise of grammar was Pāṇini's *Aṣṭādhyāyī* in the *c.* sixth to fourth century BCE. A subsequent commentary thereon, the *Mahābhāṣya*, was written by a grammarian named Patañjali in the *c.* second century BCE.[2] While the attitude of the grammarians towards language was direct referentialism – that the meaning of the word coincided with (was identical with) the object itself – most of the later schools of thought rejected or modified this view. Certainly, in later centuries the debates became polarized between the grammarians (*vaiyākaraṇas*), particularly Bhartṛhari (*c.* fifth century), who proposed that all cognition is linguistic, and the Buddhists (such as Dignāga) who proposed that cognition should be free from conceptuality, including names (Mohanty 2000: 18–19). However, across the various schools there were many disputes on these points. The earlier grammarians held that language is reality and reality is language – hence words do not just reveal or represent objects but are identical to those objects. However, there was much nuance in later theories of language, often linked to the *pramāṇas*, or valid bases of knowledge (discussed in 'Chapter 4: Epistemology').

For example, the Cārvākas (materialists), Buddhists and Vaiśeṣikas (atomists) claimed that since perception and inference exhaust all knowledge about reality, this left only a limited role for knowledge derived from language (*śabda pramāṇa*). Hence for these schools, language was not an independent means of knowledge about reality. Indeed, early Buddhists often claimed that language distorted reality. However, Buddhists and Vaiśeṣikas did accept that religious words have a role to play in knowledge and can be determined as valid/invalid through the processes of perception and inference. And, of course, although scripture (*āgama*) was not officially accepted as a *pramāṇa* by these schools, there were some adaptations so that the word of the Buddha (*buddhavacana*), for example, was the foundation of all truth claims in Buddhist thought. Even though Buddhist schools did not accept the Vedas, we can also see adherence to the authority of hearing, as in the standard opening line of the recorded sermons of the Buddha, 'Thus have I heard'. Furthermore, both Nyāya and Vaiśeṣika posited a total correspondence between language and reality (whatever is real is knowable in words). Amongst the other schools, including Sāṃkhya and Yoga, scriptural authority (*āgama/śabda/śruta*) was accepted as a *pramāṇa* and indeed was the only way to acquire knowledge about transcendent reality, since that cannot be known through perception and inference.

Language, authority and valid knowledge

One of the three valid bases of knowledge (*pramāṇa*) on which the philosophy of yoga is constructed is authority. The *Yogasūtra* refers to authority using a range of terms, depending on context: it is *āgama*, which indicates scripture, it is *śabda*, which indicates 'word' (or sound) and it is *śruta*, which indicates 'heard' (meaning reliable testimony). In each case, what is being referred to is language itself – sometimes the recorded word (in oral/written scripture), sometimes a functional grammatical consideration of language and sometimes a more abstract notion of 'the word' as indicating a metaphysical property of language. Here is the opening definition of scripture/authority (*āgama*) at PYŚ 1.7:

> Or the matter of that which has been inferred and seen by a qualified person [whose] own realization is passed on and taught using words. *Āgama* is the mental process whose content becomes the object [of understanding] for the hearer. *Āgama* is defective in the speaker who is untrustworthy, who has not seen and inferred [for oneself directly]; but when the proper speaker has seen and inferred the object, it is without error.
>
> (PYŚ 1.7)

This passage asserts several interesting philosophical points. The first is in reference to meaning and intention – intention must be present for meaning to be conveyed. The second is about fallacious or defective claims to authority; without perception or inference, no authoritative claim can be made on the basis of language alone. Hence, as a *pramāṇa*, the authority of language relies on the prior bases of perception and inference. Authoritative text also occupies a different sensory space in human cognition. In contrast to the privileging of the sense of sight as the basis of perception and inference, authority is linked to the sensory capacity of 'hearing', reflecting the archaic nature of this *pramāṇa* in oral culture and texts.

Although knowledge derived from sound/language (*śabdajñāna*) is a valid basis of knowledge, it also gives rise to other forms of knowing such as 'ideation' or 'mental construction', which is neither right knowledge nor false knowledge (PYŚ 1.9). This in-between category of ideation is key to our everyday understanding of the world – as reflected in statements such as the mundane 'Caitra has a cow'[3] or the more metaphysical 'consciousness (*caitanya*) is the nature of *puruṣa*' (PYŚ 1.9). Yet when we probe further, Patañjali says, these statements are found to be problematic with respect to 'truth', 'reliability', 'verifiabilty' and so forth. Such phrases cannot be said to describe reality as it is – yes, we can make sense of 'Caitra's cow' because we can easily grasp the difference between the two (Caitra and cow) in reality, but in the case of '*puruṣa*'s consciousness', since *puruṣa* is consciousness alone, there is a sense in which this phrase is not descriptive at all. In fact, the grammatical genitive case is entirely misleading as there are not two objects, only one. This second example is a mere mental construction of ours that does not correspond to reality (i.e. the reality of *puruṣa* as singular and beyond binary difference). Hence, there can be a gap or slippage in the compatibility between ideation based on language (or verbal knowledge) and the truth of reality. Indeed to attain the weakening of *vṛtti* (the production of thoughts) and eventually the goal of yoga as the cessation of thoughtforms, then ideation (*pratyaya*) itself must be ceased (PYŚ 1.41). There is therefore an ambiguity towards mental language (as opposed to uttered language) as a realm in which apparently true statements may be misleading.

Moreover, the *Yogasūtra* asserts that sound (*śabda*) can never be truth-bearing (*ṛtaṃbharā*), since (like inference) it can only ever point at universals and not at particulars and, as we have learned, it is only in the knowledge of particulars that one can access truth (PYŚ 1.49). This reminds us of the primacy of perception as a *pramāṇa*. Words, then, are general labels or tags for things (a 'cow' or a 'jug'), but can never signify a particular instantiation of 'this cow' or 'this jug' in the here and now. This is a fundamental limitation of language and its capacity to lead us to truth. Of course, truth also has an important moral dimension (see the discussion of truth, *satya*, as a moral restraint in 'Chapter 7: Ethics'). On this point, Patañjali even suggests that truth can be constitutive of objective reality (*prakṛti*):

> **When truth has been established, it is the foundation for the fruition of action.**
>
> (YS 2.36)

The commentary explains, somewhat naively, that whatever a person endowed with truth utters, it materializes. Hence, if one tells another person to become virtuous, they become virtuous; if one tells another to attain heaven, they go to heaven. Indeed, there is more than a hint here of the older grammatical understanding of language as direct referentialism, coupled with the notion of the cosmogonic power of language associated with Vedic linguistic concepts such as *vāc* (language), *akṣara* (primordial syllable) and *oṃ* (a specific primordial syllable). In the older Vedic worldview, language is a power that engenders reality; the whole world is created through the vibratory capacity of divine sound. In the broadly synthetic attitude of the *Yogasūtra*, Patañjali incorporates these older speculative philosophies of language with the more systematized reasoning of the later grammarians.

The Vedic practice of language

In addition to a philosophy of language, Patañjali's system also advocates a practice of language. We should bear in mind that traditional instruction of the *Yogasūtra* required it to be memorized by students through recitation. Even today in Indian universities and other educational establishments, the text is still often learnt by heart in philosophy classes. We can glimpse the roots of this Vedic system in the *Yogasūtra*'s account of language.

The active method *(kriyā yoga)* outlines recitation (of the Vedas) as one of its three key means, along with contemplation on *īśvara*. The contemplation on *īśvara* is also explained in the first *pāda* as a form of objective concentration. The method is to make *īśvara* the object of one's focus (YS 1.23). This is performed by reciting a single syllable *oṃ*, which is also called the *praṇava* (primordial syllable) (YS 1.27). The use of the term *praṇava* indicates an adherence to the closely related doctrine of the *akṣara*, or primordial syllable which in the early Vedic period was said to generate the entire cosmos.[4] Hence reality was understood to be an expression of language. Vedic conceptions of language also centred on two other key concepts. The first is a primordial creative force called *vāc* (language). Representing the whole and potential expression of language in the abstract, *vāc* was gendered as feminine and regarded as a goddess (but was not personified like other Vedic deities such as Indra, Agni or Soma).

Gradually, *akṣara* came to be an important concept, considered to be an instance of the compressed potentiality of all language in one syllable. Over time, however, the abstract understanding of *akṣara* was replaced by the conception of a specific syllabic utterance, *oṃ* (O'Brien-Kop 2014).

In Patañjali's more grammatical discussions, the extraordinary syllable *oṃ* is also subjected to the philosophical scrutiny of linguistic theory. The commentary to *sūtra* 1.23 enquires into the referentiality of this utterance, *oṃ,* posing the onto-linguistic question: is the relation between *oṃ* and *īśvara* a conventional one (i.e. arbitrary) or does it have a fixed relation (i.e. inherent and permanent) like the relation between a lamp and light. Since this point is made within the discussion of *īśvara*, it sits within a wider claim that the valid basis of knowing *īśvara* is *āgama*, or scripture. Hence this section has a special interest in language derived from scripture and, arguably, a vested interest in reifying the authority of scripture. One way to shore up scripture is to assert that the relation between meaning and word in scriptural sources is fixed, and hence that there are doctrinal truths in scripture which can be ascertained:

> The scriptural scholars assert that the relation of word and meaning (*śabdārtha*) is eternal.
>
> (PYŚ 1.27)

There is also a hint here of the older philosophy of direct referentialism, or the permanent, inherent and natural relation between words and the objects they signify.

Patañjali's system of language

The understanding of language in the *Yogasūtra* extends beyond analysis of scripture into a general theory of language that encompasses the conditions of utterance, the conditions of linguistic possibility and the reception or understanding of the utterance.

Some of the basic precepts of how language functions are laid out for us in the commentary to YS 3.17. Patañjali identifies nuanced distinctions in the components of language. For example, a distinction is made between the act of utterance (*vāc*) and the act of hearing (*śrotra*). Utterance relies on syllables/letters (*varṇa*), while hearing relies on transformations in sound (*dhvanipariṇāma*). A word (*pada*) is the binding together of vowels and consonants (*nādānu*; lit. 'atoms of sound', perhaps best translated as 'phonemes') in a form that is mentally recognizable (*buddhinirgrāhya*). Although phonemes are distinct speech sounds in themselves, existing apart from their presence in words, they are combined only in the process of a subject's hearing or understanding – words cannot form autonomously (PYŚ 3.17). Letters or syllables (*varṇa*) can, of course, be combined in myriad ways to form the multitude of words that exist, and in phonemes lies the accumulated potential of language to express all possible words (*sarvābhidhānaśaktipracita*) (PYŚ 3.17). Yet in the way that phonemes are sequenced to form a word, the difference in how the phonemes are uttered (or indeed read) is what enables the meaning of the word to emerge. Hence, in English for example, the word 'bat' is only a recognizable word because the 'a' sound is preceded by 'b' and followed by 't', and not by any other consonants – any other sequence of letters would produce a different word, such as 'cat' or 'ban'. Such recognition of phonetic differences is what makes words intelligible. Furthermore, Patañjali posits that the meaning of a word is conventionally assigned (rather than naturally inherent) and, once assigned, that meaning becomes specific. Therefore a word cannot simply refer to anything, but has a closely constrained, if not unique, meaning. The example Patañjali provides is the Sanskrit word *gauḥ*, which refers to 'an object with a dewlap', i.e. a cow, and not to any other object (PYŚ 3.17).

In addition to understanding how meaning is constructed through words phonetically, Patañjali theorizes how meaning is understood. Despite the sequencing of phonemes in a word, this is not how a word is understood – a listener/reader does not have to continually break down a word into phonemes, such as c/ow to understand its meaning. Rather, with conventional usage the meaning of a word simply appears or registers in the mind in a flash of understanding or illumination (*nirbhāsa*). One must, of course, wait for the final phoneme to be uttered (to know that the uttered word is 'coat' and not 'coated'), but once the word has been heard repeatedly, its meaning is understood instantly. Finally, mental predispositions (*saṃskāras*) as a form of prior knowledge, as well as memory (*smṛti*), contain conceptual or affective pre-judgements that form part of the conventional understanding of words (PYŚ 3.17). Hence our understanding of words is shaped, in part, by our individual lived experiences, memories and associations.

Concept, word and object

Patañjali considers the relation between concept, word and object in some detail, and proposes that the three should be properly distinguished and not mixed up. This rule also applies to the practice of meditation itself, which is geared towards correct perception of these distinct categories in order to understand the nature of reality. Often, according to Patañjali, there is an unfortunate co-mingling between a concept, word and object. Although traces of all three are necessarily present in objective meditation, the goal is to get beyond conceptual association. Hence in most of the meditation paradigms presented in the *Yogasūtra*, techniques that have traces of verbal 'handles' or labels for objects are ranked relatively lowly: such as in the progressive fourfold formula of verbal association/scrutiny (*vitarka*), apprehension (*vicāra*), joy (*ānanda*) and 'I am' (*asmitā*) (YS 1.17). *Sūtra* 1.42 provides a further indication of what *vitarka* means in this context. In the description of how the mind identifies with (assumes the form of) objects in its purview, we are told that one level of this objective concentration occurs in the state of *vitarka*, i.e. that the concentration is permeated by verbal or linguistic construction (*vikalpa*), which is the 'co-mingling of word (*śabda*), object (*artha*), and idea (*jñāna*)' (YS 1.42). The text instructs us that these three are, in fact, separate:

> the property of the word is different, the property of the object is different, the property of the idea (*vijñāna*) is different – this is the way in which they are divided.
>
> (PYŚ 1.42)

And *sūtra* 3.17 reinforces this point in the statement that word (*śabda*), object (*artha*) and *pratyaya* (mental representation or idea) are commonly confused:[5]

> **Confusion is due to the mutual imposition of word, object and idea, whereas knowledge of the sounds [utterances or language] of beings comes from meditation upon the divisions between [word, object and idea].**
>
> (YS 3.17)

These three categories can be properly distinguished by means of *saṃyama*, a type of meditation in which categorical relations are examined. This *sūtra* echoes PYŚ 1.42 in which absorption with verbal associations (*savitarka samāpatti*) is defined as a meditative condition in which word, object and idea remain intermingled. Hence, the word 'cow', the object 'cow' and the concept 'cow' are all distinct and should not be mixed up, because such conflation yields illusory knowledge (PYŚ 3.17). The promise for one who can make the correct distinctions is none other than omniscience (*sarvavit*) (PYŚ 3.17).

The theory of language on the whole tends towards a realist conception: if a word exists, then the corresponding object or state likely exists. However, the existence of an object is not dependent on words or concepts. Hence to merely utter the word 'tree' demonstrates the tendency of words to refer to real entities (PYŚ 3.17) – i.e. the fact that the word 'tree' exists indicates the prior existence of an entity 'tree'. However, the word 'tree' also contains the possibility of the sentence 'the tree exists', prompting or inferring a predicate (in this case a verbal phrase). A secondary onto-linguistic point here is that words are suggestive or indicative of sentential structure. This applies to verbs as well as nouns. Hence the verb 'cooks' implies an agent, a means (of cooking) and an object (to cook) – it carries the connoted sense of the subject 'Caitra' (a placeholder name), the means of 'fire' and the object 'rice'. Furthermore, words should not be taken at face value, and should be properly scrutinized and understood to disambiguate multiple meanings (PYŚ 3.17). In each case, the correct meaning can only be established by convention (*saṃketa*) and context (PYŚ 3.17).

A further reflection on the relationship between cognition and language lies in the discussion of determinate and indeterminate perception (see 'Chapter 4: Epistemology'). In the Sāṃkhya-Yoga view, the first type of perception to occur is indeterminate, with the understanding that this is a type of non-linguistic or pre-linguistic apprehension. Hence indeterminate (*nirvikalpaka*) perception precedes the linguistic nature of determinate (*savikalpaka*) perceptions.

Despite its nod to the archaic Vedic reverence of language as infallible, the source of reality and even divine in nature, Patañjali's approach to language is more sceptical and grounded in functional analysis. Therefore, verbal association (*vitarka*), which is derived from linguistic construction or conceptual knowledge (*vikalpa*), is dismissed as a confused state, since true knowledge of the object should strive to surpass all conceptuality and linguistic handles. As long as one resides in linguistic states, one is still relying on authority (or verbal testimony) and inference (reasoned language) rather than direct perception of the thing-in-itself (PYŚ 1.42). The concentration that rests on direct perception alone (free of linguistic construction) is known as *nir-vitarka*, free of *vitarka*. Because of the linkage between words, ideas and objects, language still binds us to the material world of *prakṛti* and to the mind, whereas the goal of the yoga system is to accomplish non-cognitive or non-objective concentration during meditation.

Negated terms and cognition of absence

There is an interesting excursus on the grammatical negative at PYŚ 2.5 in explaining the import of the word *avidyā* or nescience. Patañjali argues that although the word is formed from the negating prefix '*a-*' and the word for knowledge, '*vidyā*', we should not assume its meaning to be limited to the binary structure of 'knowledge' and 'non-knowledge'. Rather than merely indicating the negation of knowledge or the absence of knowledge, *avidyā* indicates a type of knowledge that is present in its own right, i.e. nescience:

> It (*avidyā*) should be understood as a [real] thing (*vastu*) like an enemy or a non-hoof-print. Just as 'non-friend' does not mean 'non-existent friend' nor 'the quality of a friend', but rather the opposite state, enmity; and just as non-hoof-print does not mean 'non-existence of hoof-print' nor 'the quality of hoof-print' but rather another location (*deśa*) [i.e. unmarked ground] different from both – so *avidyā* is not right knowledge (*pramāṇa*) nor the non-existence of right knowledge, but rather *avidyā* is the opposite of [right] knowledge (*vidyā*) and is another [form of] knowing.
>
> (PYŚ 2.5)

Nescience, then, not only indicates the absence of correct knowing, but constitutes a basis of knowledge in its own right, albeit wrong knowledge. More broadly in Early Indian Philosophy, the absence of knowledge is a category of knowledge in its own right, indicating a cognition of absence (such as looking into a room and noting 'the chair is not there'). This knowledge is sometimes called *abhāva* (absence). For Patañjali, nescience is not 'no knowledge', but it is a full state of knowing with positively existent misconceptions (e.g. conceiving impermanence, impurity, suffering, non-self where there is none). Again, this statement of linguistic fact indicates the difficulty of attaining right knowledge: one has to first remove the erroneous cognitions, which are often bound up with language, before right knowledge can even be introduced.

Many of the concepts of language discussed in this chapter seem strikingly modern. In philosophy of language, it seems reasonable to move from Patañjali's technical analysis to the terminology of post-structuralist linguistics: the sign (word) is made up of the signifier (utterance as a sound or word on page) and the signified (intentional meaning or concept). It is no surprise to find out that one of the founders of European linguistics, Ferdinand de Saussure (1857–1913), was a Sanskrit scholar of Indian śāstric texts – and many of his ideas on language were taken from Indian philosophy of language (Li 2018). However, we must also caution against a strictly functionalist analysis of Patañjali's theories of language. Older Vedic cosmological ideas of language are also present in the *Yogasūtra*, particularly in the notion that language is eternal and has no beginning (*anādi*). Such an assertion resonates perfectly of course with the broader eternalist metaphysics of this school.

Discussion questions

1. What is your view of the relation between word, concept and object? Do they coincide or is difference crucial? Do you find Patañjali's theories convincing?
2. Since Patañjali's philosophy of language is formulated in relation to a single language, Sanskrit, does this limit the wider applicability of these theories?
3. What differences in philosophical understanding might be produced by reading a text, hearing it, or learning to recite it from memory?

Further reading

Coward, H. (1990) *Derrida and Indian Philosophy*. New York: SUNY.

Gerety, F. (2021) 'Between Sound and Silence in Early Yoga: Meditation on "Oṃ" at Death' in *History of Religions* 60.3: 209–44.

Kaviraj, G. (1923–24) "The Concept of *Pratibhā* in Indian Philosophy." *Annals of the Bhandarkar Oriental Research Institute* Vol 5.1, 1–18.

Kunjunni Raja, K. (1977) *Indian Theories of Meaning*. Madras: Adyar Library and Research Centre.

Li, C. (2018) 'Sounding Out Différance: Derrida, Saussure and Bhartṛhari' in *Philosophy East and West* 68.2: 447–59.

Lucyszyna, O. (2017) 'On the Notion of Linguistic Convention (*saṁketa*) in the *Yogasūtrabhāṣya*' in *Journal of Indian Philosophy*, 45.1, 1–19.

Matilal, B. K. S. (1990) *The Word and the World: India's Contributions to the Philosophy of Language*. Oxford: Oxford University Press.

Raghuramaraju, A. (2019) 'Derrida and the Two Forms of the Word: Writing West and Speaking India' in Raghuramaraju, A. (ed.) *Calibrating Western Philosophy for India: Rousseau, Derrida, Deleuze, Guattari, Bergson and Vaddera Chandidas*. London and New York: Routledge.

7

Ethics

Chapter outline

If ethics is, as Perrett states, fundamentally concerned with two questions, 'What ought we do?' and 'Why ought we do it?' (Perrett 2007: 149), then Patañjali's *Yogasūtra* is an ethical text par excellence. A primary function of the text is to instruct on *dharma*, how to live a good and virtuous life, according to yoga philosophy precepts. It also provides a clear rationale for its ethical frame, both in terms of justification and authority from tradition, but also in terms of the benefits of the goals set out, the ultimate of which is liberation or existential freedom. The *Yogasūtra* has a fully developed ethics that includes the major elements we would expect: 'a set of first-order moral precepts, a consequentialist theory of the right, and a theory of the good' (Perrett 2007: 149).

Moral retribution: The theory of *karma*

In line with the broader concerns of Indian philosophy, the *Yogasūtra* grapples with the moral problem of action (*karma*), in that to act can result in harm, to oneself or others. According to the pan-Indian theory of *karma*, actions are not only motivated by mental intentions, but also in turn condition mental dispositions that produce future actions of a similar kind, thus creating a seemingly inescapable loop. These predispositions were thought to form a layer or stratum of the mind:

> Thence the karmic substratum of merit and demerit is produced by desire, delusion, and anger.
>
> (PYŚ 2.12)

Mostly, the driving motivations for action are, as identified above, the 'afflictions' (*kleśa*s), which are packaged in two ways. One model explains the mental afflictions as fivefold: nescience (*avidyā*), egoity (*asmitā*), attachment (*rāga*), aversion (*dveṣa*) and fear of death (*abhiniveśa*) (PYŚ 1.8) (see also 'Chapter 4: Epistemology'). Another model, frequently found in Buddhist sources, describes the afflictions as 'poisons' (*viṣa*s) or 'faults' (*doṣa*s) in a threefold formula: desire (*rāga/lobha*), delusion (*moha*) and aversion (*dveṣa*) (YS 2.12).[1] Hence we can say that this worldview promotes a rather pessimistic conception of human action as having a propensity towards wrong action. It requires the great effort of living a life aligned to *dharma* to swing the balance towards good actions (e.g. YS 2.14). However, on the whole, a sense of natural justice prevails in the way that karmic retribution is explained. There is a like-for-like equivalence between the act and the effect of that act on the agent: hence if one causes harm to another, they will experience commensurate harm themselves, if not in this life then in a future life, or indeed in a hellish dwelling (PYŚ 3.34). *Sūtra*s 2.35 to 2.45 lay out the direct equivalence between good action and moral outcomes, with an internal-external trajectory: for example, for one established in non-harm, all violence (around them) dissipates (YS 2.35), one established in contentment experiences utmost bliss (YS 2.42) and so forth.

The theory of *karma*, as laid out by Patañjali, is a complex system that has much moral nuance. Moreover, the personal fabric of moral retribution (*karma*) is not homogenous in nature. *Karma* has a latent quality, but, according to kind, it can manifest quickly or slowly (PYŚ 3.22), in this lifetime or across multiple lifetimes. Certain kinds of *karma* shape future incarnation in different ways – such as determining one's next lifespan (PYŚ 3.22).

First-order moral precepts

For contemporary yoga practitioners the world over, one of the best-known sections of the *Yogasūtra* are the first two stages or auxiliaries of the eightfold system (*aṣṭāṅga yoga*). These two stages explain ethical precepts that are often still applied (or interpreted) by today's yoga practitioners (religious or secular) to cultivate a moral foundation for leading a 'yogic life'. Of course, there is a gap between the early social context of Patañjali's *Yogasūtra* and the variegated contemporary social contexts in which its precepts are now practised. Nonetheless, as an ethical code, the applied value of these precepts is extraordinary in its popular reach and appeal for global audiences today. The moral precepts of Patañjali's system are used to inform and underpin all kinds of social engagement and ethical standpoints – from environmental activism to anti-consumerism, social justice, animal ethics and so-called 'conscious capitalism'.[2]

What are these explicit ethics? The first stage of the eightfold system of practice is a set of standard precepts called the restraints (*yama*s), which are social or relational (and together comprise the *mahāvrata*, or great vow) (YS 2.30–2.31):

ahiṃsā (non-harm)
satya (truth)
asteya (non-stealing)
brahmacārya (continence/celibacy)
aparigraha (non-grasping)

The second set of precepts are observances (*niyama*) that reorient the ethical focus to the individual (YS 2.32). These practices are about self-discipline:

śauca (purity/cleanliness)
saṃtoṣa (contentedness)
tapas (asceticism)
svādhyāya (recitation or study of scripture)
īśvarapraṇidhāna (contemplation on *īṣvara*)

Some scholars have analysed the *yama*s and *niyama*s as don'ts and dos respectively. The order of these two distinct sets of five principles is suggestive. First, we see a progression from a more relational practice in the *yama*s (self in relation to 'the other') towards a narrowing focus to one's own self and body in the *niyama*s. Second, we see a progression from more universal or abstract values (such as truth) to more specific, embodied and practice-based values, in this case associated with Vedic tradition (such as recitation of texts). Indeed, the first set of precepts, the restraints, have a more universal quality – and this is not surprising since they were also shared by Buddhists and Jains.

In Buddhism, these five precepts are referred to as *śīla*, or moral conduct, and are commonly found in early Buddhist literature in which *śīla* is usually the preparatory practice for meditation. Similarly, one of the oldest surviving Jain texts, the *Ācārāṅgasūtra* (*c.* third to fourth century BCE), describes ascetic regimens to reduce one's *karma* and lists five precepts which are identical to Patañjali's five *yama*s. It is worth dwelling on Jain ethics here, since they, in some measure, shaped the moral outlook of the *Yogasūtra*.

In Jainism, the five precepts collectively constitute the great vow (*mahāvrata*), support the elimination of *karma* and propel one towards existential liberation (*mokṣa*). Non-harm or *ahiṃsā* was particularly central for Jains in which the path of practice was accomplished only when all worldly impacts of action (karmic traces) were eradicated. Liberation for Jains was technically understood as *kevala*, a state of perfect and pure isolation of the self (*jīva*), freed from the weight of moral impurity. Asceticism (*tapas*) and meditative absorption (*dhyāna*) culminated in the complete renunciation of attachment to one's own body, a practice called *kāyotsarga* (Pragya 2020). The Pātañjala theory of *karma* is further indebted to Jain notions on moral action in the declaration that residual 'dark *karma*' (demerit) is eradicated by the 'rise of bright *karma*' (merit) in this current lifetime (PYŚ 2.13). Patañjali's description of the colours of *karma* as black, white or black and white (YS 4.7) echoes the Jain idea that *karma* is a material substance that has different colours (*leśya*) to reflect distinct types or grades of moral action. In these reckonings of the balance-sheet of good and bad in the world, then, we can see that the early Indian theories of action were not so pessimistic after all; although humans have a propensity towards wrong actions, there was great belief in the efficacy and power of virtuous action to set the world to right.

In the *Yogasūtra*, the precepts are introduced as part of the eightfold method (*aṣṭāṅga yoga*) that is designed to destroy erroneous perception (*viparyaya*) in order to cultivate correct knowledge (*samyagjñāna*). The ultimate goal of morality is cognition, which subordinates correct conduct to correct knowledge (or ethics to epistemology). We might say that the ethical precepts themselves are purposive, i.e. they are designed to support the process of attaining liberation, rather than absolute values in themselves. In this respect, the ethics of the *Yogasūtra* are not necessarily deontological, or absolute codes with intrinsic value. One exception to this observation, however, is the principle of non-harm (*ahiṃsā*), the foundational precept of moral restraint. PYŚ 3.31 points out that in Brahmanism there are many traditional exceptions to the rule of non-harm, in which it might be one's duty to carry out harm – such as by occupation as a fisherman or as a participant in a prescribed ritual sacrifice.[3] However, such justifications for harm are rejected in the *Yogasūtra*: for the accomplished *yogin*, non-harm is to be practised 'among all beings, among all objects, on all sides and without any deviations and on all levels' (PYŚ 2.31: trs. Larson 2018: 545). There is therefore no context in which harm can be justified, and this is the foundational principle of the entire system of Pātañjala ethics.

As we have seen, the centrality of non-harm for Patañjali reflects a universal ethical code shared by the three major philosophical communities of Brahmanism, Buddhism and Jainism. However, the *Yogasūtra* also situates its ethics in relation to Vedic culture and belief by adding the observances (*niyama*s). Purification is both outward cleansing of the body and pure diet, but also purification of the mind and of ordinary awareness (PYŚ 2.32). Asceticism indicates the capacity to endure bodily austerity, fasting and vows of silence. Recitation is study of texts that explain liberation, or repetition of the syllable *oṃ*.[4] Contemplation of *īśvara* occurs only when one has sufficiently destroyed karmic seeds and obstacles in the mind that blight correct perception (PYŚ 2.32). Indeed *sūtra*s 2.33 and 2.34 delineate the practice of how to remove the obstacles: when unvirtuous thoughts arise they must be countered with a virtuous thought (selected from the above *yama*s) which will have the effect of neutralization. However, even though it is culturally situated in relation to the Vedas, and proposes *īśvara* as an ambiguously theistic figure, the *Yogasūtra* is a resolutely non-theist text, and it is solely human agency that drives one's fortunes across one or more lifetimes.

Finally, a word on the *pramāṇa*s. In 'Chapter 4: Epistemology', we discussed how the system of the *Yogasūtra* starts and ends with epistemology – theories of knowing, knowledge and truth. We have already assessed the end goal of the *Yogasūtra* as epistemological, to exist in a state of pure knowing (pure consciousness, *puruṣa*). Unsurprisingly, the ethics of Patañjali also rest on epistemology; like all forms of knowing the truth, the precepts are subjected to the baseline of the three *pramāṇa*s of perception, inference and authority (PYŚ 2.30). In the case of the five observances (*niyama*s), however, there is a particular link to the authority of the Vedas (PYŚ 2.30), thus highlighting the relation between normative conduct and prescriptive text.

The principle of non-harm

It has long been noted that the origins of the principle of non-harm, foundational to all the restraints (*yamas*), most likely had its roots in the renouncer (*śramaṇa*) movements of Jainism and Buddhism rather than Brahmanism. In the Vedic period, Brahmanism (early Hinduism) permitted harm as a sanctioned part of ritual sacrifice. Rukmani situates the stance of the *Yogasūtra* in this wider context of Vedic ritual in which animal sacrifice was condoned as a sometimes necessary principle of harm. She concludes that the categorical rejection of harm on any count in both the *Yogasūtra* and the *Sāṃkhyakārikā* was therefore 'courageous' (Rukmani 2011: 138).[5] Arguably, these Sāṃkhya-Yoga positions were being established in a period of social flux – the Vedic mores were giving way to more nuanced discussions, as evidenced in moral dilemmas foregrounded in the epic *Mahābhārata* (in both the 'Bhagavad Gītā' and 'Śāntipārvan' sections) which explore the moral choices of harm and non-harm in relation to social duty and the greater good.[6] Nonetheless it is still significant that the *Yogasūtra* offers an unambiguous position on non-harm, wherein it is prohibited without qualification. An (unattributed) quotation underlines this absolute principle and makes a moral assertion that may seem unfamiliar to contemporary readers, that one's pleasure or enjoyment entails suffering for others:

> Furthermore it has been said: 'Enjoyment is not produced without hurting living beings, so there also exists a bodily layer (*śarīraḥ*) of karmic deposit (*karmāśaya*) that is produced by violence'.
>
> (PYŚ 2.15)

This notion (that pleasure is morally wrong) exists within a backdrop of asceticism and provides a strict affirmation of the moral superiority of renunciation as a lifestyle of self-denial that avoids causing harm to others. Engaging with 'the right' in this ascetic philosophy entails desisting from the comforts and pleasures of life by, for example, moderating food intake (PYŚ 1.15), withstanding physical austerity such as extremes of temperature (PYŚ 2.48) and so forth.

Patañjali's text is not only clear on the primacy of non-harm as the foundation of all moral action, but also asserts that the (circular) purpose of the ten restraints and observances is to achieve non-harm itself (PYŚ 2.30). In short, each of the moral precepts that follows *ahiṃsā* in the formula of the *yama*s is an enjoinment based on the harmful effects (to others) of any such action: falsehood, theft, non-chastity and insatiable attachment. Such harms are both social and personal, physical and psychological. Indeed, this point is elaborated further in PYŚ 2.34 where we encounter a fascinating taxonomy of harm (*hiṃsā*): levels of violence intersect with other states of non-virtue to produce a complex prism of harmful effects in the world. Although there are eighty-one sub-divisions of harmful acts in which triad axes of agency (done/caused/approved), type (greed/anger/delusion) and level (mild/medium/extreme) are mapped against each other, we are told that in the end the varieties of harm are 'innumerable' (PYŚ 2.34). Hence, for most scholars, Patañjali's instructions have an important consequentialist dimension; there is an abundance of clarity on what we ought not to do and on what we ought to do. As moral precepts, the restraints (*yama*s) and observances (*niyama*s) form counterstates to moral failings that produce harm in the world and, as such, should be positively cultivated at every opportunity, since they are instrumental in attaining liberation.

There are, however, some interesting questions in relation to the motivation towards and pursuit of liberation. Yoga philosophy is not a socially oriented theory of liberation, but highly centred on the individual and on an end goal that is the isolated ontological state of pure consciousness. Indeed, PYŚ 4.33 informs us that not everyone can attain liberation at once because of the eternal nature of *saṃsāra*, which is therefore endless. In short, suffering and bondage will always exist. Hence:

> A good person, having achieved proper understanding, having destroyed or overcome all desires, is not reborn; but another (lacking the qualities of the good person) is reborn.
>
> (PYŚ 4.33: trs. Larson 2018: 965)

Furthermore, liberation is not positively framed in terms of 'bliss' or 'happiness' (as in other traditions, e.g. Advaita Vedānta or Buddhism). Pleasure only produces the existential problem of desire or craving (YS 2.7):[7]

> Certainly, he who is a pleasure-seeker (*sukhārthī*), in the thrall of sense objects (*viṣayānuvāsita mahati*), is sunken in the mire of suffering, like one who is afraid of the scorpion poison but gets bitten by a venomous snake.
>
> (PYŚ 2.15)

The value of cultivating merit through self-denial or pain (asceticism) is, in part, intrinsic in that it is inherently dharmic. However, *dharma* (virtuous conduct) is also simply a necessary means to attain the goal of liberation. Hence PYŚ 2.15 tells us 'For the discriminating one (*vivekinaḥ*), all is suffering alone'. This might seem like a bleak worldview, but as the commentary explains, the pursuit of happiness or pleasure is not a goal of this system:

> In all cases, the experience of happiness is penetrated with attachment, depending on causes that are both animate and inanimate – thus there exists karmic deposit (*karmāśaya*) born of attachment [...] And the objects of happiness (*sukha*) are said to be nescience (*avidyā*).
>
> (PYŚ 2.15)

It is only by accepting suffering as the unavoidable condition of life that one can begin to cultivate virtue. (There are, of course, echoes here of the Buddhist worldview.) How, then, in a world in which happiness has no intrinsic moral worth can humans be motivated to follow a strict ascetic code? And can these philosophical ideas speak to contemporary subjects for whom the pursuit of pleasure (e.g. as consumers) is often an embedded part of material existence?

There are, in fact, some concessions to happiness, such as at PYŚ 2.28 where we are told that *dharma* is the cause of happiness in the way that *aṣṭāṅga yoga* is the cause of disjunction from impurity (i.e. from *adharma* or non-virtue). Moreover, even the happiness of contentment (*saṃtoṣasukham*) is only suffering in comparison to the happiness of isolation (*kaivalyasukham*) (PYŚ 3.18) (isolation here indicates residing in pure consciousness). However, on the whole, liberation in the *Yogasūtra* is framed as negative ontology, as an absence of the suffering that pervades all material life (YS 2.15). An absence of suffering (as we discussed in 'Chapter 3: Ontology') is indicated as a disembodied liberated state (*videhamukti*) – possibly, but not necessarily, post-death. Yet the question remains as to whether this is a sufficiently positive or attractive goal to provide people with the motivation to engage with 'the right' in a consequentialist frame.

And yet some practical rewards are guaranteed for virtuous moral conduct: following the convention that concentration on an object generates an ontological identity with the essence of that object, the same is promised for affective states. Hence, we become what we think about and, according to the contemplative formula of YS 1.33, the act of focusing on friendliness (*maitrī*), compassion (*karuṇā*) or joy (*muditā*) towards others produces the very presence and power of this affect within the practitioners themselves (PYŚ 2.23). Other rewards are less easy to understand rationally, but are part of the contemporaneous worldview that advanced meditation practices yield extraordinary mental capacities (YS 3.16–49). Perhaps such intermediate states of disembodied freedom (through perfected sensory capacities, or *siddhi*s) provide a kind of pragmatic motivation for those who need it (to justify sitting in fixed absorption, *dhāraṇā*, for long periods). In comparison, the more abstract and final goal of disembodied and contentless consciousness makes a less appealing basis for leading a life of denial based on 'the right' and 'the good'. These pragmatic outcomes (the positive affect of extraordinary capacities) offer an attractive counterpart to the foundational precept that all life is suffering. Indeed, when one recognizes that life is dissatisfactory (such that even happiness is tinged with pain) one will naturally start to dissociate from it, resulting in a radical and ultimate detachment that constitutes 'the good', and the highest value. Yet because the ultimate 'good' (isolated consciousness, *kaivalya*) is largely framed in terms of absence (apophatically), the presentation of morality as consequentialist is more convincing than deontology as a model of how ethics drives the *Yogasūtra* – even if the figure of *īśvara* as a perfect or ideal figure goes some way towards building a virtue ethics.

Ranganathan has an interesting theory on why *ahiṃsā* is foundational to Pātañjala ethics and not truth (which ties in to his view of the *Yogasūtra* as first and foremost a work of ethics).

> Putting *ahimsā* first is to privilege objectivity over truth: when we do not harm, we allow for the objectivity of things in our environment, including ourselves and other people, as self-determining objects in the world.
>
> (Ranganathan 2017: 190)

Patañjali's text supports this view. Truth should be for the sake of helping other beings, and should truth ever be uttered with a harmful intention or produce an injurious effect on others, then it would be morally wrong (*pāpa*) to do so (PYŚ 2.30). Truth, considered in this way, is not so much absolute as relational.

Environmental ethics

So far, we have considered how Pātañjala ethics condition one's moral conduct towards oneself and other human beings. But what of one's moral attitude to non-human beings or nature? Given the current environmental crisis, these are ethical issues that have become increasingly important for contemporary readers of the *Yogasūtra*. Arguably, the overall metaphysics of the text, in which nature (*prakṛti*) exists for the sake of consciousness, does not bode well for certain facets of environmental ethics, such as environmental stewardship. Such gendered metaphysics may be seen to reinforce the gendered tropes of anthropocentricm that reify disparity and appear to grant permission to exploit nature. However, there are many nuances in how the *Yogasūtra* is interpreted for the context of the environment. Recently, several scholars have put forward readings of the *Yogasūtra* as a text through which one can constructively address environmental and animal ethics in our contemporary world.

For example, Framarin argues that plants and animals have both sentience and moral standing (2014: 149) and that, because of the theory of reincarnation (i.e. that one may be reincarnated as a plant or an animal), plants and animals are living entities that continue to exhaust their karmic accrual more efficiently than humans. This is because they are not engaged in moral action in the way that humans are (i.e. actions that continue to generate new karmic accruals which bind humans further to *saṃsāra*) (Framarin 2014: 134). Hence, the pain and death that animals and plants experience expedites their exhaustion of karmic accrual, implying that 'animals and plants generally make steadier progress toward *mokṣa* than human agents do' (Framarin 2014: 149). Such an argument has interesting implications for contemporary environmental ethics in which we might consider that humans' participation in environmental degradation and meat consumption are morally demeritorious actions that further delay a human's existential liberation, even while plants and animals move closer to it (in that they expedite their karmic elimination more quickly).[8]

Individualism and social ethics

Reading the *Yogasūtra* can generate a moral dilemma regarding the principles of dispassion (*vairāgya*) and practice (*abhyāsa*), in that both appear to promote individualism. In this text, dispassion is a principle of detachment of the individual self from one's material and social environment, while practice is a principle of cultivation of the self. Does such a disproportionate focus on the self preclude a concern for the social? The argument can be made that the text employs social ethics (the five *yamas*) only as an instrumental basis by which to purify and cultivate the self, rather than an engagement that is designed to lead to the social good as a valid goal in itself.

Ranganathan (2017) makes an insightful contribution in this regard, in his assessment of the *Yogasūtra* as offering a sophisticated moral theory and 'an ethical alternative to Deontology, Consequentialism and Virtue Ethics'. He argues:

> Yoga is hence a missing ethical theory from the usual spread we learn about in the Western tradition.
>
> (Ranganathan 2017: 177)

Like Framarin, Ranganathan agrees that moral standing applies to any entity that can thrive if given freedom, and hence covers not only human beings, but also 'most animals, and the Earth' (2017: 177). Such a theory of 'personhood', according to Ranganathan, is 'non-speciesist' (177–8). Further, unlike the liberalism of John Stuart Mill, which is entangled with 'the ugly side of Western culture: speciesism, paternalism, or imperialism' (178), yoga offers a moral theory that is 'truly liberal' (179). In addition to western ethical frameworks of consequentialism, virtue ethics and deontology, Ranganathan proposes a new moral understanding derived from the *Yogasūtra*, one which he terms '*bhakti*' – indicating the broad principle of 'devotion' to an ideal (182–3):

> devotion to an ideal defines a normative practice, and the perfection of this practice is the good.
>
> (2017: 183)

There are some points of critique here – mainly that Ranganathan's somewhat theistic account of morality as synonymous with *bhakti* is itself reliant on a theistic 'interpretation' of a Sāṃkhya philosophy that declares itself non-theistic and a yoga philosophy that addresses theism in a lukewarm manner (see 'Chapter 2: Metaphysics'). Secondly, the *Yogasūtra* does not itself feature the word '*bhakti*', and Ranganathan's theory appears to be addressing a wider body of texts that would include the *Bhagavad Gītā*. Moreover, his framing of yoga philosophy as anti-teleological is also open to discussion, since arguably any system that sets up existential freedom and pure consciousness as an end goal also justifies a means to attain it. However, beyond these general points, what is most striking and useful about Ranganathan's reading is that, for him, the *Yogasūtra* is on the whole an ethical system. Even *samādhi*, the end goal of perfected concentration, is understood as an 'ethical state of absorption' – thereby shifting analysis from the more usual ontological, epistemological or soteriological understandings of this term (185). Hence, freedom is a virtue which indicates 'isolation from determinism', i.e. from *prakṛti* (187). For Ranganathan this radical ethics is about 'autonomy', i.e. *kaivalya*, and rather than indicating a transcendent goal, the outcome of this philosophy is the more prosaic capacity to 'self-govern' (193) and to be 'self-determining' (194).[9] In Ranganathan's estimation, people (and the definition of personhood here can include non-human and human animals),[10] if left to such 'unconservative' self-governance (i.e. if granted radical autonomy), will naturally gravitate towards virtue:

> if we give people the room to be people, we find that they often start to live the virtuous life: non-harm, faithfulness to the uncoerced facts, respecting property, not hoarding, and sexual restraint (the Great Vows).
>
> (2017: 194)

Ranganathan's statements prompt several questions, such as why a natural moral order should reflect the five precepts of the *Yogasūtra* rather than other possible moral frameworks, or the confidence with which radical individual autonomy is claimed to lead to a social good (apart from through the respect accorded to the other, detailed in the five precepts). Rejecting consequentialist or deontological models as inappropriate to describe Patañjali's ethics, Ranganathan settles on 'virtue ethics' as the best descriptor of what it is to follow the regulative ideal of *īśvara* (what Ranganathan calls 'lordliness') (2017: 195–9). There are important political dimensions in Ranganathan's analysis that highlight the virtue of a just and equal society and a world in which non-human animals are not harmed. However, his conclusion as to the ethical merits of renunciation may present an overly optimistic solution to the problem of social harm:

> As the yogi causes no threat to the prevailing practices that cause evil, but merely opts out, she will live peacefully with evil, long enough to make a difference.
>
> (2017: 199)

With respect to the environment, time, unfortunately, is not on humanity's side, and with respect to human populations, textual interpretations of ethics are not equally weighted in terms of social power.

Yoga, politics and power

A further important arena in which contemporary readers of the *Yogasūtra* are redeploying the text's adherence to non-harm is that of social justice and political activism. Such projects often use the foundational principles of Patañjali's ethics to query how the system of yoga has been used to perpetuate various ills of social exclusion or privilege in history or in today's world – for example in relation to class, gender or race. From time to time, the PYŚ addresses its direct audience as Brahmin males (e.g. PYŚ 2.30, PYŚ 4.29), reflecting the restricted social access to this Sanskrit text for much of South Asian history. However, the social dynamics of yoga in the contemporary world are even more complex.

Vital current discussions centre on the necessity of decolonizing yoga, since in global knowledge transmissions, white western audiences have selectively adapted elements of South Asian heritage, such as yoga, and decontextualized it through cultural appropriation, while at the same time vilifying other aspects of South Asian culture (Black 2020). The ethics of commercializing yoga have also been critiqued (Godrej 2017; Jain 2015), and we can add that the quest to commodify the *Yogasūtra* for profit by (over)emphasizing its practical dimensions has rested on erasing the philosophical as well as the religious meanings of this text – an erasure that this present book seeks to address in part. Such commercialization of the yoga episteme has reinforced class privilege through monetized participation that has made access to and hence knowledge about yoga exclusive on the basis of financial affordability.

However, the *Yogasūtra* also occupies a constructive role in social justice movements in that the self-care offered by the text's practices – i.e. to focus on and to cultivate the self – can also provide moments of respite from the efforts of political activism, such as anti-racism, as well as opportunities to build safe community spaces. The text itself, then, has a meta-ethical role in today's world in that it not only contains ethics (and provides an ethical blueprint), but is also transactional in broader contemporary social ethics – for good and bad. The *Yogasūtra* can be understood to contribute to the perpetuation of institutions such as white supremacy and neoliberal capitalism, but also to offer tools for ethical reorientation towards positive disengagement from society (anti-consumerism, mental respite) and positive engagement with society that can produce solidarity for oppressed or marginalized groups.

Discussion questions

1. Reread the ten ethical precepts (the restraints and the observances). Can these be regarded as providing a relevant ethical framework for contemporary readers of the *Yogasūtra*? Or is re-interpretation and adaptation necessary?
2. What do you make of the *Yogasūtra*'s argument that enjoyment and pleasure entail causing harm in the world?
3. In relation to ethical debates, such as those pertaining to the environment or social justice, how might a more philosophical understanding of the *Yogasūtra* contribute constructively?

Further reading

Black, S. (2020) 'Decolonizing Yoga' in Newcombe, S. and O'Brien-Kop, K. (eds.) *The Routledge Handbook of Yoga and Meditation Studies*. London and New York: Routledge.

Chapple, C. (2018) 'Jaina Ethics and Moral Philosophy' in Bilimoria, P. (ed.) *History of Indian Philosophy*. Routledge History of World Philosophies. London and New York: Routledge.

Framarin, C. (2014) *Hinduism and Environmental Ethics: Law, Literature and Philosophy*. London and New York: Routledge.

Godrej, F. (2017) 'The Neoliberal Yogi and the Politics of Yoga' in *Political Theory* 45.6; 772–800.

Jain, A. (2015) *Selling Yoga: From Counterculture to Pop Culture*. Oxford: Oxford University Press.

Mohanty, J. N. (2000) 'Moral Philosophy' in *Classical Indian Philosophy*. Lanham: Rowman and Littlefield.

Perrett, R. (2007) 'Sāṃkhya-Yoga Ethics' in Bilimoria, P., Prabhu, J. and Sharma, S. (eds.) *Indian Ethics: Classical Traditions and Contemporary Challenges Volume 1*. London and New York: Routledge.

Pragya, P. (2020) 'Jain Yoga' in Newcombe, S. and O'Brien-Kop, K. (eds.) *The Routledge Handbook of Yoga and Meditation Studies*. London and New York: Routledge.

Ranganathan, S. (2017) 'Patañjali's Yoga: Universal Ethics as the Formal Cause of Autonomy' in Ranganathan, S. (ed.) *The Bloomsbury Research Handbook of Indian Ethics*. London and New York: Bloomsbury Academic.

8

The aesthetics of freedom

Chapter outline

This chapter further situates the *Yogasūtra* in its context as a *sūtra* text, highlighting its formal literary aesthetic: conciseness, clarity, condensation and an elegant coherence of ideas. Like other texts of its time, Patañjali's philosophical conceptuality rests on metaphors, similes, analogies, narrative illustration and other literary devices. Given the text's status as a *śāstra*, its vestigial adherence to direct referentialism (the belief that word and object coincide)[1] and its partial roots in oral recitation, there is an inextricability of the literary form, genre and aesthetic from the text's meaning. However, beyond the formal integrity of the text, the *Yogasūtra* also promotes a unique aesthetic of freedom: a system of mind-body philosophy that is simple, organized and uncluttered. This aesthetic is so engrained in the text's reception history that it is one reason why the *Yogasūtra* has endured across millennia into contemporary transglobal contexts. I argue that Patañjali's text demonstrates a coherence between the literary, conceptual and embodied aesthetic that is a feature of Indian philosophical thought.

This chapter is a short one, since the concept of the aesthetic in the *Yogsūtra* has not been widely discussed and aesthetics is not an explicit topic on Patañjali's agenda. Yet there is something to say about the formal aesthetic of this text and its ideal of freedom, represented as a pure, contentless consciousness (*puruṣa*). Between the form of the *sūtras*, their content (the ideas and systems) and the goal of the liberated state, there is a consistent emphasis on the pared down and the minimal as the marker of the ideal, and hence of beauty. There is a resonance, then, between the soteriological aesthetic, which is characterized by light and steadiness or constancy, and the textual aesthetic, which holds a beauty in the elegant simplicity of its format as aphorisms but also in the steady, logical unfolding of precepts (the thread of reasoning). We will also consider the antonymic state of the reviled and abject, often associated with mere physicality itself – for in a text in which pure consciousness is freedom, then embodiment is bondage.

Bodily aesthetics: Embodiment and abjection

Patañjali's system does not subscribe to the notion of the physical body as an object of beauty. Rather, in true ascetic fashion, the body is always an object of impurity and disgust – almost without exception. As the *sūtra* 2.5 on the erroneous cognitions informs us (mistaking what is impermanent, impure, painful and not-self to be permanent, pure, happy and self), it is an error to perceive purity in the 'impure, the utmost disgusting body' (PYŚ 2.5). This admonition is followed by a quoted verse:

> 'Because of its state, its origin, its excitation, its emissions, its death, and its need to be purified, *paṇḍits*[2] know the body to be impure.'
>
> (PYŚ 2.5)

These lines reveal the attitude of ascetic austerity that permeates this yoga philosophy; it is a world-renouncing tradition that rests on the abjection of the body in the pursuit of a higher goal of realizing the nature of consciousness. The text instructs on how the physical body can be cleaned with water and other natural substances. Moreover, by maintaining a pure diet, fasting or austere physical practices one can attain mastery over the body to withstand extremes (of hunger and thirst, cold and hot, standing and sitting, and types of silence) (PYŚ 2.32). From such purity arises abhorrence or disgust (*jugupsā*) with one's own body and avoidance of contact (*saṃsarga*) with the bodies of others – and one becomes an ascetic (*yati*)[3] (PYŚ 2.40).

Conventional poetic or romantic descriptions of corporeal beauty, particularly feminine beauty, are vilified as wrong convictions:

> Because in the impure, purity is perceived. It is as when a young girl might lead [one] to love – like the crescent moon, her limbs as if made from honey and nectar, appearing as though sent forth from the moon, with eyes like the petals of the blue lotus, she consoles the living world with alluring gestures and glances [...] Thus there exists in impurity the erroneous idea of purity.
>
> (PYŚ 2.5)

In an ascetic method designed by, narrated and systemized by men, such tropes of feminine beauty are merely a false aesthetic, and these stock examples are used to expose the pitfalls of female bodies. Desire or grasping as the basis of existential suffering is understood not only as a mental phenomenon, but also as a physical one (i.e. the pleasures of the immanent world, *kāmaloka*). The commentary to YS 2.42 cites the *Mahābhārata* on this point:

> Whatever happiness from the fulfilment of desire (occurs) in the world, and whatever happiness (occurs) in the magnificence of heaven, these are not even a sixteenth portion of the worthy (Yogin), whose happiness occurs in the destruction of thirsting (*tṛṣṇā*).
>
> ('Śāntiparvan' 12 168.36: Belvalkar 1954)

There is one uncontested image of corporeal beauty, however, and this is the austere bodily form of the ascetic: the diamond body (also a familiar trope in Buddhist soteriology).

> **The perfected body (*kāyasaṃpat*) is graceful, strong and diamond hard.**
>
> (YS 3.47)

So, despite its propensity for impurity, the body and senses can be perfected through yoga practices (YS 2.43). In places, the text offers a constructive view of how the dimensions of the body might prove useful. PYŚ 3.29–34 details how direct contemplative knowledge of different bodily zones (the navel, the heart, the throat) yields special forms of cognition.[4] These can lead to supernatural capacities such as clairvoyance, supersensory audition and transforming one's body to be minute and to transcend space (PYŚ 2.43). This perfected body, *kāyasaṃpad* (PYŚ 3.45–47), operates in a state of ideal freedom with regard to materiality – a body that can move through space, matter and time unimpeded in any way. It is important to note, however, that this perfected body is merely a stage on the way to existential freedom in which the body, ultimately, does not figure, only consciousness. In the aesthetic of emotion, it is not love that is the ultimate state, but rather a form of anti-affect (i.e. not embodied), supreme detachment:

> Dispassion (*vairāgya*) is the highest limit of knowledge. For isolation (*kaivalya*) is inseparable from it.
>
> (PYŚ 1.16)

The ultimate form of detachment is the liberated state, what might be called transcendental aloneness.

Mental aesthetics: Constancy and light

Throughout the text, the supreme virtue is steadiness (*sthiti*), which is thwarted by inconstancy. Although the body must be cultivated in relation to steadiness, the most beautiful object is the steady mind which, in its stillness, allows the natural qualities of luminosity and transparency to be apparent. The stated goal at the outset of the *Yogasūtra* is the cessation of mental modifications, *vṛtti*s (YS 1.2). The counter to these natural virtues of constancy and luminosity are the obstacles. The obstacles are defined as 'distractions' (PYŚ 1.29), and there is a sense in which cognitive distraction is a moral failing in itself, because it undermines the affective state of steadiness. In a system geared towards concentration, this figures, since physical steadiness (*āsana* or seat) is a prerequisite for concentration. Hence stillness is valued above all forms of fluctuation, modification, wavering or movement. The commentary introduces *sūtra* 1.30 as follows:

> Now these obstacles are the confusions of the mind. What are they and, moreover, how many?
>
> **1.30 The obstacles that are confusions of the mind are disease, sloth, doubt, error, idleness, non-abstension, confused knowledge, non-attainment of the levels, incapacity to remain.**
>
> These nine obstacles are the confusions of the mind. They exist with the fluctuations of the mind. When they do not exist, the previously mentioned modifications of the mind do not exist. Disease is the distress of the humours, fluids, and organs. Sloth is the ineffectiveness of the mind. Doubt is knowledge (*vijñāna*) that touches both sides [in an argument], saying 'it might be this or it might not be this'. Error is the non-existence of the practice (*sādhana*) of concentration (*samādhi*). Idleness is the inactivity of the body and mind due to heaviness. Non-abstension is the greed (*gardha*) of the mind by the yoking of objects to the self. False knowledge is erroneous cognition. The condition of non-attainment of the levels is not attaining the stages of *samādhi*. Incapacity to remain is non-steadfastness of the mind in the level of attainment. Upon the obtaining of *samādhi*, it (mind) would be stable. These nine mental confusions are considered impurities of yoga, enemies of yoga, obstacles of yoga.
>
> (PYŚ 1.30)

In contrast to these distractions, concentration must be established, one-pointed, grounded and steadfast, which refers to both body and mind. YS 1.29 tells us that distractions in the body manifest as pain, agitation and trembling or shaking limbs; furthermore breath – as an intermediary between body and mind – is also subject to this principle, because distraction results in spasmodic or confused breathing patterns (YS 1.29). The role of the body is merely as a vehicle through which to perfect the mind: 'Then the mind or *citta* (=*buddhi*) that is arrived at "I-ness" manifests only "I-ness" that is infinite, peaceful, like the motionless great ocean' (PYŚ 1.36). The beauty of the sattvic mind is only evident when it becomes an ocean of stillness, but this too must be left behind in the pursuit of freedom.

In addition to steadiness, the ideal state is expressed via recurring metaphors of light. The expression of light in materiality is evident in the *guṇa* of *sattva*. The *yogin* begins to apprehend one's own clear and luminous nature by cultivating sattvic *buddhi* which 'is free from the dirt of obstacle and impurity' and is 'a steady, transparent flow that is not overpowered by *rajas* and *tamas*' (PYŚ 1.47). However, beyond *sattva*, the ultimate form of light is the unwavering luminosity of consciousness itself. Indeed, the journey of the adept towards liberation is marked not only by the increasing incline towards the lightness of *sattva*, but also in the decreased density or weight in one's being. The first indication of a loosening of the relation between body and mind (indicating the diminishing importance or weight of the body) is mental self-awareness, such that one can start to project the mind beyond the confines of the body (PYŚ 3.38, 3.43). For example, an identification (*saṃyama*) with light leads one to the most light forms of matter: one can walk on the threads of spiders webs and dissolve into sunbeams (PYŚ 3.42). The clarified *buddhi*-mind shines forth (*nirbhāsate*) like a luminous jewel, like a crystal (PYŚ 1.41). The inherent aesthetic in these descriptions is one of light. Therefore, in answer to the question 'What does existential freedom look like?', we might answer, 'It is a disembodied state wherein all material identity has been dissolved and only the light of consciousness remains.'

Literary aesthetics: The poetics of simple form

Here, I would like to consider how the formal literary aesthetic of the *Yogasūtra* conveys a poetics that is entirely in accord with the philosophical goal of Patañjali's system – in that less is more.

Classical Indian poetics included theories of metaphor, as part of the classification of linguistic and literary stylistic devices known as *alaṃkāraśāstra* (precepts of ornamentation). The earliest formal works on Sanskrit poetics were Daṇḍin's *Kāvyādarśa* and Bhāmaha's *Kāvyālaṃkāra*, both *c.* eighth century (Tzohar 2018: 5 fn 5). Prior to these systematizations of literary devices was Bharata's treatise on aesthetics, the *c.* fourth-century *Nāṭyaśāstra*. Yet there is no extant formal or consistent theory of metaphor (or even of figurative language more generally) in Indian literature – philosophical or otherwise – in the early common era (Tzohar 2018: 5; 25). Indeed, metaphors are often subtly embedded in *sūtra* texts, rather than being deliberately and showily crafted according to the rules of *alaṃkāraśāstra*. More relevant to a philosophical discourse like Patañjali's, then, were accounts of metaphor that we find in the śāstric works of the grammarians. Pāṇinī's *Aṣṭādhyāyī*, for example, describes four grammatical aspects of comparison: the subject of comparison (*upameya* or *upamita*), the comparand (*upamāna*), the property of similarity (*samānya* or *samānadharma*) and the grammatical indicator of comparison (*sāmānyavacana* or *dyotaka*) (*Aṣṭādhyāyī* 2.1.55.6; 2.3.72; 3.1.10).

In different literary cultures, poetry is understood as a form that is semantically saturated, i.e. more information is condensed than in ordinary language. This is a statement that can also be made about the *sūtra* format. Observations about the poetic form are useful in considering how metaphoric condensation works in the *sūtra* format. Poetry is a stratified system in which meaning only exists contextually, and a poetic text has a unique kind of internal organization (Lotman 1976). These statements are also applicable to the *sūtra* textual format. The meaning of a *sūtra* only exists contextually in relation to the supplied commentary (*bhāṣya*); a *sūtra* text is uniquely bound by context in that it cannot make sense alone, without its relational commentary, whether oral or written. Furthermore, a *sūtra* text has a unique internal organization compared to other textual formats of the period. Contracted argument forms are laid out in logical order as major premises, sub-premises and supporting detail. The conciseness of the *sūtra* format is primarily a mnemonic device, but it is certainly also designed to lead to precision of meaning (even though for contemporary readers the act of reading often produces greater indeterminacy of meaning).[5] Poetry and the *sūtra* format thus share minimum redundancy and maximum condensation.

Given this conciseness, metaphors become an ideal way to convey large amounts of information using minimum words. The power of metaphor is in the rich field of association that it generates, including connotational fields.[6] To capture a whole field of meaning in a *sūtra*, one cannot but resort to metaphors. Metaphors condense literal meaning into imagistic nexi that convey whole clusters of meaning in just one phrase. Although the poetic format dispenses with all the usual markers of communication as redundant (i.e. poetry is often concise expression), it nevertheless has to convey a rich set of messages. A poem is typically complex and condensed at the same time, which means that all the stratified levels of meaning cannot be apprehended at once. This led Lotman to argue that that a poem cannot be read, only re-read. His observation is relevant when considering the mnemonic function of the *sūtra*; it is designed to be re-membered (with its commentary) and reiterated (verbally recited or philosophically pored over, time and time again).

This point can perhaps be better understood by employing select analysis from modern linguistic theory. The linguist Jakobsen (drawing on de Saussure, who we might remember was also a scholar of early Sanskrit texts) theorized that a sentence has two axes of operation through which meaning is produced (Jakobsen 1956). One axis is 'horizontal' in that words are linked in a sequence to make sense grammatically; this is called the 'syntagmatic' axis of meaning and is all about how words are combined for effect. The other axis is 'vertical' in that each word we use could be substituted by an infinite number of other words with similar or opposite meanings; this reflects the paradigmatic axis of sentences in which word selection occurs, and it is associated with metaphor. In compositions where brevity is the key principle, such as poetry or a *sūtra* text, any sentence pushes each word to convey the breadth and depth of syntagmatic and hidden paradigmatic structures of meaning – both grammar and metaphor are pushed to their limits.[7]

When we add to such condensation in syntax the 'additional' layers of meaning generated by the *Yogasūtra*'s overall formal structure (with its logical conventions and structures of argumentation), then the complexity and profundity of conceptual information is only increased.[8] Hence a *sūtra* text is dense. Anyone who has read or, indeed, tried to translate the *Yogasūtra* will know how long it can take to grasp the meaning of a single aphorism, be that because of the condensation of grammar that occurs (e.g. YS 1.36 **'Or existing in sorrowless luminosity'**) or the deeper meanings inferred in just one image. A single condensed image such as the 'cloud of dharma' or a 'diamond body' is a doorway into a world of profound meaning, often criss-crossing other thought systems such as Buddhism and Jainism, the luminous depths of which are quietly signalled by the steadily threaded beads of knowledge.

Arguably, the *Yogasūtra* is a text of deceptive simplicity. It is designed to be read and re-read in context, and on each reading (in a hermeneutic circle) further strata and webs of meaning become apparent, adding to philosophical understanding through the practice of reading and rational reflection.

Discussion questions

1. Do you agree with the text's positioning of constancy and light as the highest aesthetic values? How does this compare to other aesthetics that you have studied?
2. In a system that appears to devalue the body as abject, how does Pātañjala yoga philosophy intersect with the aesthetic of the body in yoga-related worldviews today?
3. Is the *Yogasūtra*'s textual brevity and conceptual condensation a source of beauty or obscuration? Could it have been designed to be both?

Further reading

Chakrabarti, A. (ed.) (2016) *The Bloomsbury Research Handbook of Indian Aesthetics and the Philosophy of Art*. London and New York: Bloomsbury Academic.

O'Brien-Kop, K. (2020) 'Dharmamegha in Yoga and Yogācāra; The Revision of a Superlative Metaphor' in *Journal of Indian Philosophy* 48.4.

Patton, L. (2008) '*Ṛṣis* Imagined across Difference: Some Possibilities for the Study of Conceptual Metaphor in Early India' in *The Journal of Hindu Studies* 1: 49–76.

Patton, L. (2013) 'Poetry, Ritual and Associational Thought in Early India and Elsewhere' in Patahak, S. (ed.) *Figuring Religions: Comparing Ideas, Images and Activities*. New York: SUNY.

9

Conclusion

This book has sought to position the *Yogasūtra* as a philosophical work with rich veins of ideas about the human condition that are still of value some 2000 years after the work's composition. In scholarly and broader popular representations, the *Yogasūtra* has often been foregrounded as a practice manual or a religious text. It does, of course, convey religious ideas and practices, but, mostly, as the title *sūtra* indicates, it is a work of systematic philosophy. Indeed, reading the *Yogasūtra* along with its first commentary highlights its philosophical scope, because the commentarial explanations of the *sūtra*s reveal more of the philosophical underpinnings.

Even within the academic study of Indian philosophy, the *Yogasūtra* is sometimes accorded less attention than other root texts of the six *āstika* schools, coloured as it is by related and later conceptions of yoga as a physical practice. Yet a philosophical reading of the text and its commentary situate it within the realm of 'classical' ideas and arguments and reveal it to be a useful intertext with which to read other texts, not only the *Sāṃkhyakārikā*, but also, for example, the *Vaiśeṣikasūtra* and the *Brahmasūtra*. Scholars (such as Larson and Bhattacharya) have often approached the text from within the discipline of religious studies, or within the historical frame of indological study (e.g. Maas). This has led to deep historical contextualization, as well as important analysis of the text as philosophy of religion. Yet, there is something to be said for recent scholarship that has approached the text more directly and exclusively from within the discipline of philosophy. I have tried to weave in some of those contemporary philosophical framings (e.g. Ranganathan, Funes Maderey, Ashton) because I think they unlock more of the ideas and arguments in the *Yogasūtra* than we have hitherto dealt with in anglophone scholarship.

As for religion, Patañjali's *sūtra*s are not theistic on the whole, nor does the text foreground *dharma* as a central concern. Resting as it does on non-theist Sāṃkhya (which in some respects is as close to Buddhism as to Hinduism), Patañjali's ideas about self, consciousness and one's place in the world are relatively malleable in relation to doctrine. This, in part, explains why yoga philosophy has had a non-sectarian history in South Asia (and has been tied to traditions as varied as Pāśupata yoga, Tibetan Buddhist Vajrayāna and Vaiṣṇava devotion). The text's relatively neutral stance on 'God' also explains why it continues to have broad resonance for global secular audiences today.

Above all, what I hope to have conveyed in this book is that the method proposed by Patañjali is not physical practice, since sitting (*āsana*) is a preparation for meditation, which is rational reflection. Recognizing the *Pātañjalayogaśāstra* as a work of systematized philosophy requires sustained efforts from us, the readers, in order to engage with its often abstract rationality. Yet the text nonetheless anchors such abstractions in staged sequences of rational reflection that are more easily grasped. Such contemplation is directed towards understanding the different categories of reality and leads to profound comprehension of the mind, consciousness, self, nature and freedom. Again, the resonance of this text for our age can be linked to these specific dimensions of personhood. In an era in which material progress has produced increased psychological stress, the text appears to offer insights into techniques to improve mental health. Such responses may, in part, be anachronistic, since mental health is a neologism, and Patañjali's clear goal is 'truth' rather than 'happiness' as such. Yet, if the text supports enquiry into contemporary questions about human values and identity, how the mind works, and how mental stability or balance is to be achieved, then these are surely important goals of any philosophical system.

Beyond these contexts, I hope that this book has highlighted the academic value of reading the *Pātañjalayogaśāstra* as a logically underpinned treatise, a comprehensive package of ideas, a systematized worldview. Patañjali's text is a major work of philosophy and in its endurance in a global forum has proved as popular and wide-reaching in its influence as any work by Plato. It therefore merits inclusion as a key text on philosophy degree programmes – not as an adjunct to add a smattering of world philosophies to a Eurocentric curriculum, but as an integral work of philosophy in its own right. The methods of engaging with the systematized philosophies of global cultures can be demanding – a 'fusion of horizons' requires us to question the presuppositions in our own epistemic frame, to bracket certain assumptions and to engage in new forms of synthetic thinking (Gadamer 1995/1960). We are also asked to embrace alterity by thinking into concepts that may be unfamiliar to our worldview (*karma*, reincarnation, time as cyclical), to accept the limited translatability of certain ontological categories (*puruṣa*, *prakṛti*), to extend our conceptual comfort zones and even to learn new languages. But the endeavour of world philosophies cannot be meaningfully engaged without a decentring or provincializing of the western episteme (Chakrabarty 2000). This entails a deconstruction of the hegemony of the universal, so that epistemology is pluralized, and diverse and polycentric knowledge systems are actively employed in the doing of philosophy. The *Yogasūtra* of Patañjali can be a productive partner in this philosophical process.

Glossary of key Sanskrit terms

These are the main technical Sanskrit terms discussed frequently in this book. Other Sanskrit terms are glossed in each chapter. Translations below indicate the primary context in which these words are discussed in this book, but meanings will vary in other specific contexts.

abhyāsa – practice
adarśana – nescience; wrong knowledge
adharma – non-virtue
āgama – scripture, authority, testimony
ahaṃkāra – egoity
ahiṃsā – non-harm
akṣara – primordial syllable
aliṅga – unmanifested [matter], (lit. 'without mark') [synonyms *avyakta, mūlaprakṛti, pradhāna]*
anātman – non-self
anumāna – inference, reasoning
apavarga – liberation
artha – object; purpose
asaṃprajñāta – non-cognitive, non-objective (concentration)
asmitā – sense of 'I', I-am-ness
aṣṭāṅga – eightfold; eight-auxiliary
āstika – orthodox; adherent (to Vedic authority)
ātman – self
avidyā – nescience, ignorance; one of the root problems of existence and of the self
avyakta – unmanifest (in relation to matter) [synonyms *aliṅga, mūlaprakṛti, pradhāna*]
bhūmi – stage, ground
buddhi – awareness; intelligence
citta – mind
cittamātra – mind-only or consciousness-only; name of a Buddhist Yogācāra philosophy
darśana – philosophy; lit. seeing or sight

dhāraṇā – fixed mental focus
dharma – ethical or religious conduct; virtue; also entity
dharmin – individuated substance, e.g. gold or clay
dhyāna – meditative absorption
draṣṭṛ – the seer
dravya – substance (as a principle or ontological substrate)
dṛśya – the seen
duḥkha – suffering
guṇa – ontological quality
hāna – escape (from *saṃsāra*)
hetu – reason, means, cause
hiṃsā – harm, violence
jīva – self or 'soul', in Jainism
jīvanmukti – liberation while living
jñāna – knowledge, idea
kaivalya – ontological isolation
karma – action; theory of moral retribution
kleśa – mental affliction
kriyā – action
liṅga – mark (manifest feature)
manas – mind (mundane)
mithyājñāna – wrong knowledge
moha – delusion
mokṣa – liberation, emancipation (existential)
mūlaprakṛti – root or base matter (i.e. unmanifested; primordial) [synonyms *aliṅga, avyakta, pradhāna*]
nāstika – heterodox; lit. non-adherent (to Vedic authority)
nirodha – cessation
nirvāṇa – cessative liberation; enlightenment (in Buddhism primarily)
nirvicāra – non-apprehensive [concentration]
niyama – ethical observance
nyāya – logic, reasoning
pāda – chapter
pariṇāma – change; transformation
pradhāna – primordial matter (or energy); unevolved matter [synonyms *aliṅga, avyakta, mūlaprakṛti*]
prajñā – wisdom or insight
prakṛti – materiality

pramāṇa – valid basis of knowledge
prāṇāyāma – breath control
prasaṃkhyāna – enumerative reflection
pratiprasava – material involution/devolution
pratyakṣa – perception
pratyaya – ideation, mental representation, concept
puruṣa – consciousness; (also *kṣetrajña* 'the knower of the field')
pūrvapakṣa – opponent's position
rajas – dynamic quality (one of the three *guṇas*)
śabda – word; authority
samādhi – concentration; perfected concentration
saṃprajñāta – cognitive, objective (concentration)
saṃsāra – cycle of rebirth
saṃskāra – predisposition
saṃyama – identification (in meditation)
śāstra – treatise
satkāryavāda – Sāṃkhya tenet that the effect pre-exists in the cause
sattva – light or balanced quality (one of the three *guṇas*)
sūtra – aphorism; text genre; lit. 'thread'
svarūpa – essence
tamas – inert or dense quality (one of the three *guṇas*)
tāpa – pain
vāc – utterance, speech, language
vairāgya – dispassion
varṇa – syllable, letter
vicāra – subtle apprehension
videhamukti – liberated, disembodied state
viparyaya – erroneous perception
vitarka – verbal association
vivekakhyāti – discriminating discernment
vṛtti – mental process, thought process, mental operation
yama – ethical restraint

Notes

Chapter 1

1 For recent discussions on globalizing and decolonizing philosophy see, for example, Ganeri (2016), Maldonado-Torres et al. (2018) and van Norden (2019).

2 The first use of the term *śāstra* was in the *c.* fourth century BCE in the Sanskrit grammarian Yāska's *Nirukta* (1.2, 14), and *śāstra* subsequently indicated a treatise that explains the Vedas and their ritual practices.

3 Doxographers are scholars who organize and often rank historical schools of thought, such as philosophy. Much of what we now understand of the 'infrastructure' of ancient philosophy are later reckonings.

4 Some scholars reject the term 'school' because it suggests that these communities were organized in discrete or institutional ways, which may be overstating the case.

5 One exception here is the *Sāṃkhyakārikā*, which is in a verse format (*kārikā*) rather than an unmetered format (*sūtra*).

6 This school also informally incorporates the Upaniṣads and the *Bhagavad Gītā* as root texts.

7 There are divergent views on the dating of the *Yogasūtra*, ranging from *c.* second century BCE to fourth century CE. It is not the aim of this book to investigate matters of dating or authorship, but rather to focus on the philosophical ideas. For dating, see Maas 2020b: 969 fn 21.

8 *Ārṣaṃ siddhadarśanaṅaṃ ca dharmebhyaḥ.* 'Cognition of advanced sages, as also vision of the Perfected Ones, (results) from *dharma* or merits' (VS 9.2.13; trs. Sinha 1923: 294).

9 Maurya period, fourth–second century BCE; Gupta period, fourth–fifth century.

10 The Vedas is the foundational textual corpus of Hindu thought dating from approximately 1500 BCE to 200 BCE.

11 The Jains adhered to the *jīva*, self, as the ultimate principle of the universe.

12 For a discussion of the meanings of *yogācāra*, see O'Brien-Kop 2021: 79–88.

13 It does not, however, reflect the arduous physical self-negation and abjection of, say, the Pāśupata path of yoga, which was also deeply philosophical and based on the reasoned taxonomy of Sāṃkhya. For a recent discussion, see Jonker 2021.

14 There are a number of English translations of the *Yogasūtra* and its first commentary combined. See, for example, Woods (1914), Baba (1976), Rukmani (1981–89; 2001), Leggett (1990), Larson (2018). Maas produced a new critical edition of the first *pāda* and its commentary (2006).

15 Some critical editions feature 196 aphorisms.

16 This is glossed at 2.32 as study of *śāstra*s that deal with the topic of liberation (*mokṣa*) or repetition of the syllable *oṃ*.

17 These special faculties are called perfections or attainments (*siddhi*s). Such attainments entail special forms of knowledge about the cosmos as well as supernatural acquisitions such as invisibility, atomization, possession of other beings and superhuman strength. These special cognitive attainments have sparked much scholarly debate as to how they should be read on the spectrum of literal to symbolic, but it is clear that they represent a mixture of altered states of mind and profound shifts in awareness, as well as the more conventional notions of supernatural feats in the religio-philosophical discourse of the time.

18 In Hinduism, the closest model to this is the sixfold method (*ṣaḍāṅga yoga*) as outlined in brief in *Maitrī Upaniṣad*, which includes discrimination (*tarka*) as a key technique, and also in Pāśupata literature. These sixfold models appear to be historically prior to the Pātañjala formulation.

19 It is also tempting to see a reflection of the three primary methods of yoga in the three constituents of reality (*guṇa*s): '*Sattva* has the character of light. *Rajas* has the character of action. *Tamas* has the character of fixity' (PYŚ 2.17), referring to *a/saṃprajñāta samādhi*, *kriyā yoga* and *aṣṭāṅga yoga* respectively. The *guṇa*s are discussed in 'Chapter 2: The world and reality'.

20 There are two branches of Jainism: Śvetāmbara (white-clad) and Digambara (sky-clad).

21 *kāyavāṅmanaḥkarma yogaḥ*.

Chapter 2

1 For Burley, the two primordial principles are a pure subjectivity of consciousness (*puruṣa*) and a mediated subjectivity of experience (*prakṛti*), and so *puruṣa* and *prakṛti* are two parts of a larger threefold complex of pure subjectivity/mediated subjectivity/pure objectivity. I discuss this view in 'Chapter 1: Introduction'.

2 Indeed, Bronkhorst argues that philosophical systems such as Sāṃkhya and Vaiśeṣika were closer to Buddhism, particularly Sarvāstivāda Buddhism, than Vedic thought (Bronkhorst 2006: 287–90).

3 See Ashton (2020) on the Kashmir Śaiva Pratyabhijñā interpretation of the Sāṃkhya tradition.

4 *Kriyā yoga* itself means the yoga or method of 'action' – as reflected in the activities of physical austerity (*tapas*), Vedic recitation (*svādhyāya*) and contemplation on *īśvara* (*īśvarapraṇidhāna*). The notion of action here also points to the Brahmanic mode of the householder (socially engaged) rather than the more renunciatory modes of Buddhists and Jains (socially disengaged).

5 There are some statements in the commentary that suggest a one-way dependency on the part of *prakṛti*, such as explaining the cause of continuation at PYŚ 2.28 as the way that mind (*prakṛti*) depends on (is caused by) consciousness (*puruṣa*), like the body depends on food for sustenance. It may be that this simile is simply poorly chosen, contradicting as it does the tenet that pure consciousness has no content and so could not be 'food' for *prakṛti* as well as contradicting the tenet that there is no explicit causal interaction between these two phenomena of reality. However, more likely here is the doctrine that the proximate light of consciousness is a reason for *prakṛti* to evolve, which includes the production of 'mind'.

6 We do not, for example, need to take the following statement to be idealist in order to understand its meaning. Rather, it is simply pointing out that subjective perception is a cause for the construction of meaning: 'In a similar manner, the sight of the same woman may cause ignorance to someone confused, discomfort to someone in pain, passion to someone aroused, detachment to someone who truly understands the complexities of all human relationships' (PYŚ 2.28; trs. Larson 2018: 526).

7 Another instance of the low social status of women and the androcentric perspective of the text is to be found at PYŚ 1.15; the lack of detachment and self-mastery is evidenced in one who cannot resist visible objects such as women, food and drink.

8 See *Ṛg Veda* 1.164.20–2, *Śvetāśvatara Upaniṣad* 4.4.6 and *Muṇḍaka Upaniṣad* 3.1.1.

9 In the *c.* eighth-century *Yogasūtrabhāṣyavivaraṇa*, Śaṅkara is the first commentator to argue that materiality and consciousness are ultimately united in *brahman*. The arguments as to whether or not the *Vivaraṇa* can be attributed to Śaṅkara and dated this early are both controversial. For the claim that the *Vivaraṇa* was a *c.* eighth century composition by Śaṅkara, see Leggett (1990) and Harimoto (2014). For the counterargument that the text is as late as the eleventh–fourteenth century, see Rukmani (2001), and Larson and Bhattacharya (2008).

10 Such as Kṛṣṇa in the *Bhagavad Gītā*, Śiva in the *Pāśupata Sūtra* or Devi in the *DevīMahātmya*.

11 Maturation here indicates the fruits of action that 'ripen' over time, according to the theory of karma.

12 There are some resonances here with the Buddhist concept of the *bodhisattva*.

13 They can enter into rock, water does not wet them, fire does not burn them, wind does not move them (PYŚ 3.45).

14 *Nimitta* or *nimittakāraṇa* is an agent that brings a thing into being or which initiates a change. The agent is often understood as a deity.

15 In fact, this macro-process of material expression and dissolution has a counterpart in the formation of the material self and its ideal dissolution through the technique of *pratiprasava* (or reversal of the material process).

16 The term *dharma* here resonates with Buddhist philosophical usage of the term to indicate entity. More specifically, as discussed below, it can indicate properties of an entity.

17 *cūrṇamṛtpiṇḍamṛdghaṭamṛtkapālamṛtkaṇamṛd*.

18 The theory he reworks is by the Sarvāstivāda Buddhists, the claim that the progression of time is an illusion and that the past, present and future all exist in the present moment.

19 We have already discussed this passage but it is worth reconsidering here: the seen object (*dharma*) is like a magnet to consciousness and functions

by means of proximity, and in the very fact of it being seen by *puruṣa*, the object becomes the property of *puruṣa* (is owned by *puruṣa*), in that its purpose of existing is for the sake of consciousness (PYŚ 2.15; PYŚ 2.21). For similar ideas on the non-caused nature of consciousness and the limited causal frame of *prakṛti*, see SK 9–10.

20 The doctrine is evident in the statement: 'everything is contained in everything' (*sarvam sarvātmakam*) at PYŚ 3.14 in a refutation of the Buddhist three times theory. The doctrine is also apparent at PYŚ 4.3: 'no cause operates by means of its effect' (*na kāryeṇa kāraṇaṃ pravartyata*).

21 *Jāti* in Sāṃkhya-Yoga indicates species or kind.

22 *ayutasiddhāvayavabhedānugataḥ samūho dravyam iti patañjaliḥ etat svarūpam ity uktam.*

23 This is a specific use of the word *dharma* in ontology. It is drawing on Buddhist usage of *dharma* as entity, but co-exists in the text alongside other prevailing meanings of *dharma*, such as moral conduct or religion.

24 One of the synonyms for *puruṣa* is the owner or possessor (*svāmin*) of *dharmins* or *dṛśya* (PYŚ 2.22–23) – again reflecting a gendered and feudal relation between *puruṣa* and *prakṛti*.

25 I have amended Larson's translation to add an 's' to 'run'.

26 *tajjayād vatsānusāriṇya iva gāvo asya saṃkalpānuvidhāyinyo bhūta prakṛtāyo bhavanti.*

27 For the subjection here to truly be meaningful, it must be sited in the true subjectivity of pure consciousness, *puruṣa*.

28 A *dharmin* is a 'substantive substrate that supports the *dharma*' where *dharma* is the entity of Buddhist discourse or a property of an entity (Larson 2018: 998).

29 See Larson's translations (2018) of *dharma-lakṣana-avasthā* as empirical characteristic, temporal mode and change in overall condition. Maas translates them respectively as property, temporal characteristic mark and state (Maas 2020).

30 This is referred to more frequently in other philosophical schools as *dravya*, substance. And '*dharmin*' is more distinct in Pātañjala Yoga.

Chapter 3

1 Compare BG 6.41.
2 *Sūtras* are shown in bold and commentary in non-bold.
3 Rather: settling, calming and purifying the body is a gateway to mental practices.
4 'But he who curbs the senses with his mind and then practices self-control in action using his faculties of action without any attachment stands out [from the rest]' (*Bhagavad Gītā* 3.7 trs. Malinar 2012: 67).
5 *Vijṇāna* is part of the fives aggregates (*skandhas*) that make up non-self, is one of the twelve stages of dependent co-origination and is the sixth element (*dhātu*).
6 This appears to be a general critique of Buddhist thought rather than a specific critique of the so-called idealist school known as 'Mind-Only' (Vijñānavādins or Yogācāras), such as we see in the section on mind-only ontology (*cittamātra*) in the fourth *pāda*. (I discuss such critiques in 'Chapter 5: Logic'.)
7 See discussion of substance (as substrate *dravya* and individuated *dharmin*) in relation to entity (*dharma*) in 'Chapter 2: Metaphysics'.
8 See the archaic death-as-liberation image of the ascension of the self in a chariot to pierce the solar disc in the Vedic Upaniṣads and the epic *Mahābhārata* (White 2009).
9 *sā tu puruṣakhyātiparyavasānāṃ kāryaniṣṭāṃ prāpnoti, caritādhikārā nivṛttādarśanā bandhakāraṇābhāvān na punar āvartate* (PYŚ 2.24).
10 *Citta* is used both as a synonym for *buddhi* but also to capture the various levels of mind together (including *manas* and *ahaṃkāra*) – discussed in 'Chapter 4: Epistemology'.
11 This is just to remind us that *dharma* is used in three different contexts in the PYŚ. In discussions on ontology, it means entity or object, but it can also mean property of an object. In other discussions it can mean virtuous conduct, code of conduct or ethics.

Chapter 4

1 *buddher eva puruṣārthāparisamāptir bandhas tadarthāvasāyo mokṣa iti.*

2 'For the purpose of perceiving *pradhāna*, and for the purpose of *puruṣa's* aloneness, the two [come together] like the blind and the lame; that conjunction is creation, emergence' (SK 21; trs. Burley 2007: 168).

3 To add some related technical terms, *prāmāṇya* is the property of being a true cognition, and cognitions can be *pramā* (true) or *apramā* (untrue).

4 'The seer (*draṣṭā*) is *puruṣa*, witness of *buddhi*. The seen (*dṛśya*) is all entities (*dharmas*) that appear in *buddhi-sattva*' (PYŚ 2.15).

5 The seen (*dṛśya*) consists of objects and senses, both gross and subtle (PYŚ 2.18).

6 The superiority of perception is also discussed in PYŚ 1.42 and 1.43.

7 The Vaiśeṣikas include testimony (*śabda*) and comparison (*upamāna*) under inference.

8 See 'Universals and particulars' in 'Chapter 2: The world and reality'.

9 *eta eva svasaṃjñābhis tamo moho mahāmohas tāmisro 'ndhatāmisra iti.*

10 Even in the account of the five senses, they are all understood to operate within the field of perception to produce *grahaṇa* (grasping or perception) of an object (PYŚ 3.47).

11 Cf. SK 51.

12 This broad model can also be seen in *abhyāsa* (practice) and *vairāgya* (dispassion).

13 And yet there is a hint that this knowledge might be transcendental at YS 3.54: 'Knowledge arising from discrimination is liberated, all-encompassing, all pervading, and timeless'.

14 For the association of *brahman* and *ātman* with the heart, see BU 4.4.22. For the orienting of the mind to the heart, see SvUp 2.8–10.

15 Such as focusing on the image of a white lotus in the heart region as part of objective meditation (PYŚ 1.36).

16 '*Citta* has three *guṇa*s because of the disposition [*śīla*] of inertia/constancy, activity and clarity.'

17 The 'cloud of *dharma*' is a metaphor to denote the superlative state of liberation (O'Brien-Kop 2020).

Chapter 5

1 The *Sāṃkhyakārikā*, for example, opens with the topic (the removal of the threefold basis of suffering, SK 1), the means (discrimination and discernment, SK 2), the *pramāṇas* (SK 4) and so forth. The *Nyāyasūtra* opens with the topic (the 16 *padārthas* or ontological categories, NS 1), the goal (release from suffering, birth, faults and wrong knowledge, NS 2), the *pramāṇas* (NS 3) and so forth.

2 ***Samādhi pāda*** **(Chapter on concentration)**

1.1 ***atha yogānuśāsanam***
1.2 ***yogaś cittavṛttinirodhaḥ***
1.3 ***tadā draṣṭuḥ svarūpe 'vasthānam***
1.4 ***vṛttisārūpyam itaratra***
1.5 ***vṛttayaḥ pañcatayyaḥ kliṣṭākliṣṭāḥ***
1.6 ***pramāṇaviparyayavikalpanidrāsmṛtayaḥ***
1.7 ***tatra pratyakṣānumānāgamāḥ pramānāṇi***
1.8 ***viparyayo mithyājñānam atadrūpapratiṣṭham***
1.9 ***śabdajñānānupātī vastuśūnyo vikalpaḥ***
1.10 ***abhāvapratyayālambanā vṛttir nidrā***
1.11 ***anubhūtaviṣayāsaṃpramoṣaḥ smṛtiḥ***
1.12 ***abhyāsavairāgyābhyāṃ tannirodhaḥ***
1.13 ***tatra sthitau yatno 'bhyāsaḥ***
1.14 ***sa tu dīrghakālanairantaryasaṃskārāsevito dṛḍhabhūmiḥ***
1.15 ***dṛṣṭānuśravikaviṣayavitṛṣṇasya vaśīkārasaṃjñā vairāgyam***
1.16 ***tat paraṃ puruṣakhyāter guṇa vaitṛṣṇyam*** **(Maas 2006: 1–46).**

3 ***viparyayo mithyājṇānam atadrūpapratiṣṭham.***

4 ***heyaṃ duḥkham anāgatam.***

5 ***Sādhana pāda*** **(Chapter on practice)**

2.1 ***tapaḥ svādhāyeśvarapraṇidhānāni kriyāyogaḥ***
2.2 ***samādhibhāvanārthaḥ kleśatanūkaraṇārthaś ca***
2.3 ***avidyāsmitārāgadveṣābhiniveśāḥ kleśāḥ***
2.4 ***avidyā kṣetram uttareṣāṃ prasuptatanuvicchinnodārāṇām***
2.5 ***anityāśuciduḥkhānātmasu nityaśucisukhātmakhyātir avidyā***
2.6 ***dṛgdarśanaśaktyor ekātmatevāsmitā***
2.7 ***sukhānuśayī rāgaḥ***
2.8 ***duḥkhānuśayī dveṣaḥ***
2.9 ***svarasavāhī viduṣo 'pi tathā rūḍho 'bhiniveśaḥ***
2.10 ***te pratiprasavaheyāḥ sūkṣmāḥ***
2.11 ***dhyānaheyās tadvṛttayaḥ***
2.12 ***kleśamūlaḥ karmāśayo dṛṣṭādṛṣṭajanmavedanīyaḥ***
2.13 ***sati mūle tadvipāko jātyāyurbhogāḥ***
2.14 ***te hlādaparitāpaphalāḥ puṇyāpunyahetutvāt***

2.15 ***pariṇāmatāpasaṃskāraduḥkair guṇavṛttivirodhāc ca duḥkham eva sarvaṃ vivekinaḥ***
2.16 ***heyaṃ duḥkham anāgatam***
2.17 ***draṣṭṛdṛśyayoḥ saṃyogo heyahetuḥ* (Āgāśe 1919: 57–79).**

6 This paradigm relates to the Buddhist Four Noble Truths, discussed below.

7 It also deepens questions about structural parallels with the Noble Eightfold Path as the 'means' in the Buddhist formula of the Four Noble Truths.

8 In Gautama's *Nyāyasūtra c.* second century CE.

9 Some parts of this chapter have been reproduced from the 'Introduction' of O'Brien-Kop (2021).

10 Non-cognitive *concentration (asaṃprajñāta samādhi*), the highest attainment of *samādhi* in the PYŚ, was conventionally accepted by Buddhist authors as a meditative attainment of non-Buddhist schools (Anacker 1984: 70).

11 E.g. a refutation of the Nyāya-Vaiśeṣikas and the Sāṃkhyas in Chapter 9 of the *Abhidharmakośabhāṣya*'s 'The Refutation of a Theory of the Self'.

12 This text is not extant in Sanskrit. It rebuts the Sāṃkhyas after the Sāmkhya sage Vindhyavāsin previously won a debate with Buddhamitra. Indeed, the *Paramārthasaptati* is a refutation in 70 verses of the *Sāṃkhyakārikā*.

13 Buddhist texts often illustrate the unsurpassability of the Buddhist path by measuring it against the surpassability of the non-Buddhist paths (the path of the 'non-attainer').

14 Indeed, Larson boils this down neatly: 'there were two streams of early systematic philosophizing in India, namely Ṣaṣṭitantra of Sāṃkhya and the Abhidharma of Sarvāstivāda and Sautrāntika'; these two streams of soteriological thought were known as the *vijñāna* (knowledge-based) philosophy of Sāṃkhya and the *nirodha-samādhi* (cessative concentration) philosophy of Abhidharma (Larson 1989: 134–6).

15 Vindhyavāsin 'conflates' the two types of philosophy to create '*vijñāna*-cum-*nirodha-samādhi* philosophy' which creates 'the hybrid classical yoga philosophy' (Larson 1989: 136).

16 *kiṃcedam adarśanam nāma*? (PYŚ 2.23).

17 *ity ete śāstragatā vikalpāḥ* (PYŚ 2.23).

18 There is variation in how scholars demarcate this discussion. For example, Woods (Woods 1914) identifies the polemical section as YS 4.14–23 and Burley (Burley 2007) as YS 4.14–22.

19 There is another, complex discussion of *cittamātra* at PYŚ 4.10.

20 *tad anena cittasārūpyeṇa bhrāntāḥ kecit tad eva cetanam ity āhuḥ / apare cittamātram evedaṃ sarvaṃ nāsti khalv ayaṃ gavādir ghaṭādiś ca sakāraṇo loka iti. anukampanīyās te / kasmāt / asti hi teṣāṃ bhrāntibījaṃ sarvarūpākāranirbhāsaṃ cittam iti* (PYŚ 4.23).

21 *Vimśatikāvijñaptimatratāsiddhi*, *Triṃśikāvijnaptimatratā[siddhi]kārikā* and *Trisvabhāvanirdeśa*.

22 The *Mahāyānasaṃgraha* and *Mahāyānasūtrālaṅkāra*. Indeed, the earliest use of the stock phrase associated with this doctrine – 'these three realms are nothing but mind' (*cittamātram idaṃ yad idaṃ traidhātukam*) – occurs in a Buddhist Sanskrit text no longer extant but which was translated into Chinese in 179 CE, the **Bhadrapālasūtra*. In the **Bhadrapālasūtra*, the visualization of the Buddha face-to-face indicates that the Buddha is nothing but mind (*cittam eva*).

23 *duḥkhabahulaḥ saṃsāro heyaḥ. pradhānapuruṣayoḥ saṃyogo heyahetuḥ. saṃyogasyātyantikī nivṛttir hānam. hānopāyaḥ samyagdarśanam. tatra hātuḥ svarūpam upādeyaṃ vā heyaṃ vā na bhavitum arhatīti hāne tasyocchedavādaprasaṅga upādāne ca hetuvādaḥ. ubhayapratyākhyāne śāśvatavāda ity etat samyagdarśanam* (PYŚ 2.15).

24 The Buddha rejected two extremes. The first was *ucchedavāda*, the doctrine of annihilation, in which there is no fruition of *karma* or rebirth and in which the individual is completely annihilated at death. The second 'extreme' position rejected by the Buddha was *śāsvatavāda*, the doctrine of eternalism. Patañjali's passage, however, accepts the doctrine of *śāśvatavāda*.

Chapter 6

1 The word 'Sanskrit' is derived from *saṃskṛta* (perfected or well formed).

2 The common name Patañjali may have led to later conflation of identity between the earlier grammarian and the later author/editor of the *Yogasūtra*.

3 Caitra is a placeholder name, an 'average subject', like Joe Bloggs or John Smith.

4 According to this cosmogonic theory, *akṣara* (a generic syllable which will eventually be replaced by the instantiated syllable of *oṃ*) is a primordial linguistic utterance from which the whole of reality emanates.

5 As Burley points out, 'it is terminological inconsistencies such as this that ought to alert us to the likelihood of the YS's being a composite text' [*sic*] (Burley 2007: 190, fn 42).

Chapter 7

1 For a discussion of the metaphor of affliction in Buddhist and ayurvedic contexts, see O'Brien-Kop (2021: 52–5).

2 See Jain 2020 for a critique of the use of yoga in 'conscious capitalism' discourse.

3 This may refer to archaic Vedic ritual which included some animal sacrifice, such as the *rājasūya*, which required the ritual dismemberment of a horse.

4 *Oṃ* is discussed in 'Chapter 6: Philosophy of language'.

5 For those who wish to investigate further, she points to Gauḍapāda's commentary to *Sāṃkhyakārikā* 2 which 'unequivocally states that even if the Vedas declare that *dharma* is acquired through animal sacrifice, it is still impure' (Rukmani 2011: 137).

6 The dating for the *Mahābhārata* is *c.* second century BCE to second century CE. The entire text of 'Bhagavad Gītā' is dedicated to this moral dilemma. For relevant passages in the 'Sāntipārvan', see CCLV24; CCLVII 4; CCLXI 19; CCLXIV 17 (Belvalkar 1954).

7 Just as pain and suffering give rise to aversion and hatred (PYŚ 2.8).

8 In an essay that argues for the necessity of vegetarianism in Pātañjala yoga according to the principle of *ahiṃsā* in the eightfold system (*aṣṭāṅga yoga*), Dickstein speculates that moral reasoning for contemporary practitioners of yoga can be extended to principles such as *asteya* (non-theft) as a basis for veganism, since non-theft arguably precludes 'forcible extraction of milk, eggs and honey from animals who naturally produce and "own" these substances' (Dickstein 2017: 621).

9 See also Proferes on the early Vedic context of *yoga* as an emerging site of political self-sovereignty (Proferes 2007). Interestingly, there is an intersection here with some of the key ideas in the Sikh tradition, in which the term *yoga* is linked to personal, social and political attributes of self-sovereignty (Bhogal 2020).

10 Ranganathan rejects what he calls 'the evils of anthropocentrism' (2017: 194–5).

Chapter 8

1 Although the text formally adheres to separation of concept, word and object (discussed in 'Chapter 7: Philosophy of language'), it nonetheless enfolds techniques of Vedic recitation (*svādhyāya*) and adherence to the special ontological status of *oṃ* that reflect an archaic direct referentialism.

2 *Paṇḍit*s are experts or scholars.

3 Lit. 'striver'.

4 There is also a suggestion that the location of the mind is the heart. PYŚ 1.36 states that when one concentrates on the heart as a 'lotus' there is direct awareness of the *buddhi*. This image reflects the older Upaniṣadic truth that the mind resides in the heart (SvUp 2.8–10).

5 The commentary does not often digress into more imagistic discussions, but some are striking. One of the most poetic and surprising in its discursive length is the cosmology at PYŚ 3.26 in which the whole cosmos, and all its layers and types of beings, are extoled. In the midst of the cosmos is Earth, itself centred on the golden king of mountains, Sumeru, which on its four sides are crowned with silver, lapis lazuli, crystal and gold. Sumeru is understood to be the *mahābhārat* (the great land) itself, the Indian subcontinent with its directions shaded like the blue lotus (south), a yellow flower (north), white (east) and luminous (west). This fragrant and abundant land is called *jambudvīpa* (the peninsula of *jambu*) after the rose-apple tree (*jambu*) (PYŚ 3.26).

6 There is a distinction between what a word denotes (its obvious or literal meaning) and what it connotes (the field of associations that it throws up).

7 Within semiotics, Jakobsen innovated two 'axes' of language (tied to metaphoric and metonymic poles): the horizontal axis of the syntagmatic chain (syntax, grammar, the unit of expression itself, such as 'The adept meditates in the morning') and the vertical axis of the paradigm ('meditate' could be replaced by 'contemplate' or 'reflect' or other related words, while 'morning' evokes other absent terms such as 'dawn' or 'sunrise'). Meaning is only made by the combination and difference within these two axes (Jakobsen 1956). Hence, within the brevity of an aphorism, each word is chosen carefully to fulfil its function in order to convey utmost meaning.

8 Condensation is loss of syntactic scope.

Bibliography

Āgāśe, K. (ed.) (1904) *Vācaspatimiśraviracitaṭīkāsaṃvalitavyāsabhāṣyasametā ni Pātañjalayogasūtrāṇi, Tathā Bhojadevaviracitarājamārtaṇḍābhidhavṛttis ametāni pātañjalayogasūtrāṇi. sūtrapāṭhasūtravarṇānukramasūcībhyāṃ ca Sanāthīkṛtāni*. Poona: Ānandāśrama.

Aklujkar, A. (2017) 'History and Doxography of the Philosophical Schools' in Ganeri, J. (ed.) *The Oxford Handbook of Indian Philosophy*. Oxford: Oxford University Press, 32–55.

Anacker, S. (1984) *Seven Works of Vasubandhu: The Buddhist Psychological Doctor*. Delhi: Motilal Banarsidass.

Ashton, G. (2020) 'The Puzzle of Playful Matters in Non-Dual Śaivism and Sāṃkhya: Reviving *Prakṛti* in the *Sāṃkhya Kārikā* through Goethean Organics' in *Religions* 11.5: 221. 1–38.

Bangali, B. (trs.) (1976) *Yogasutra of Patanjali with the Commentary of Vyasa*. Delhi: Motilal Banarsidass.

Belvalkar, S. (ed.) (1954) *The Sāntiparvan. In the Mahābhārata, for the First Time Critically Edited. Volume 14–16*. Poona: Bhandakar Oriental Research Institute.

Bhogal, B. S. (2020) 'Sikhism: Yoga and Meditation' in Newcombe, S. and O'Brien-Kop, K. (eds.) *The Routledge Handbook of Yoga and Meditation Studies*. London and New York: Routledge, 226–40.

Bilimoria, P. (ed.) (2018) *History of Indian Philosophy*. Routledge History of World Philosophies. London and New York: Routledge.

Bilimoria, P., Prabhu, J. and Sharma, S. (eds.) (2007) *Indian Ethics: Classical Traditions and Contemporary Challenges Volume 1*. London and New York: Routledge.

Black, S. (2020) 'Decolonizing Yoga' in Newcombe, S. and O'Brien-Kop, K. (eds.) *The Routledge Handbook of Yoga and Meditation Studies*. London and New York: Routledge.

Bronkhorst, J. (2006) 'Systematic Philosophy between the Empires' in Olivelle, P. (ed.) *Between the Empires: Society in India 300 BCE to 400 CE*. New York: Oxford University Press.

Bronkhorst, J. (2007) *Greater Magadha: Studies in the Culture of Early India*. Leiden: Brill.

Bronkhorst, J. (2011) *Karma*. Honolulu: University of Hawaii Press.

Burley, M. (2007) *Classical Sāṃkhya and Yoga: An Indian Metaphysics of Experience*. London and New York: Routledge.

Chakrabarti, A. (ed.) (2016) *The Bloomsbury Research Handbook of Indian Aesthetics and the Philosophy of Art*. London and New York: Bloomsbury Academic.

Chakrabarti, K. (1999) *Classical Indian Philosophy of Mind: The Nyāya Dualist Tradition*. Delhi: Motilal Banarsidass.

Chakrabarty, D. (2000) *Provincializing Europe: Postcolonial Thought and Historical Difference*. New Jersey: Princeton University Press.

Chakravarti, P. (1975). *Origin and Development of the Sāṃkhya System of Thought*. Delhi: Oriental Books Reprint Corp.

Chakravarthi, R. (2001) *Knowledge and Liberation in Classical Indian Thought*. Hampshire and New York: Palgrave Macmillan.

Chakravarthi, R. (2007) *Indian Philosophy and the Consequences of Knowledge: Themes in Ethics, Metaphysics and Soteriology*. Oxford and New York: Ashgate Publishing.

Chapple, C. (2012) '*Siddhis* in the *Yogasūtra*' in Jacobsen, K. A. (ed.) *Yoga Powers: Extraordinary Capacities Attained through Meditation and Concentration*. Leiden: Brill, 223–40.

Chapple, C. (2018) 'Jaina Ethics and Moral Philosophy' in Bilimoria, P. (ed.) *History of Indian Philosophy*. Routledge History of World Philosophies. London and New York: Routledge, 399–407.

Copi, I. et al. (eds) (2011) *Introduction to Logic*. 14th edition. International (India). Pearson Education.

Cousins, L. (1992) '*Vitakka/vitarka* and *Vicāra*: Stages of *Samādhi* in Buddhism and Yoga' in *Indo-Iranian Journal* 35.2/3: 137–57.

Coward, H. (1990) *Derrida and Indian Philosophy*. New York: SUNY.

Daily Mail Online. 11 January 2017. 'They Kant Be Serious! PC Students Demand White Philosophers Including Plato and Descartes Be Dropped from University Syllabus'. https://www.dailymail.co.uk/news/article-4098332/They-Kant-PC-students-demand-white-philosophers-including-Plato-Descartes-dropped-university-syllabus.html [last accessed 24.1.2022].

Dhand, A. (2008) *Woman as Fire, Woman as Sage: Sexual Ideology in the Mahabharata*. New York: SUNY.

Dickstein, J. (2017) 'The Strong Case for Vegetarianism in Pātañjala Yoga' in *Philosophy East and West* 67.3: 613–28.

Doniger-O'Flaherty, W. (trs.) (1981) *The Rig Veda*. London: Penguin.

Dunne, J. (2007) 'Realizing the Unreal: Dharmakīrti's Theory of Yogic Perception' in *Journal of Indian Philosophy* 34.5: 497–519.

Endo, K. (2000) '*Prasaṃkhyāna* in the *Yogabhāṣya*' in Mayeda, S. (ed.) *The Way to Liberation: Indological Studies in Japan*. New Delhi: Manohar (Japanese Studies on South Asia, 3).

Framarin, C. (2014) *Hinduism and Environmental Ethics: Law, Literature and Philosophy*. London and New York: Routledge.

Frazier, J. (ed.) (2014) *Categorisation in Indian Philosophy: Thinking Inside the Box*. London and New York: Routledge.

Frazier, J. (2017) *Hindu Worldviews: Theories of Self, Ritual and Reality*. London: Bloomsbury Press.

Funes-Maderey, A. (2017) 'Between the Internal and the External: Kant's and Patañjali's Arguments for the Reality of Physical Objects and Their Independence from Mind' in *Comparative Philosophy* 8.1: Article 6.

Funes-Maderey, A. (2019) 'The Unbearability of the Male Gaze. An Exposition of Sāṃkhyan Philosophy of Embodiment through "Feminine" Phenomenological Eyes' in Howard, V. (ed.) *Bloomsbury Research Handbook of Indian Philosophy and Gender*. London and New York: Bloomsbury Publishing, 35–52.

Gadamer, H.-G. (1995/1960) *Truth and Method* (J. Weinsheimer and D. Marshall, Trans.). 2nd revised edition. New York: The Continuum Publishing Company.

Ganeri, J. (2001) *Philosophy in Classical India: The Proper Work of Reason*. London and New York: Routledge.

Ganeri, J. (2016) 'Why Philosophy Must Go Global: A Manifesto' in *Confluence* 4: 134–86.

Ganeri, J. (2017) *The Oxford Handbook of Indian Philosophy*. Oxford: Oxford University Press.

Gerety, F. (2021) 'Between Sound and Silence in Early Yoga: Meditation on "Oṃ" at Death' in *History of Religions* 60.3: 209–44.

Godrej, F. (2017) 'The Neoliberal Yogi and the Politics of Yoga' in *Political Theory* 45.6: 772–800.

Gokhale, P. (2020) *The Yogasūtra of Patañjali: A New Introduction to the Buddhist Roots of the Yoga System*. Delhi: Routledge India.

Gombrich, R. (1996) *How Buddhism Began: The Conditioned Genesis of the Early Teachings*. London: Athlone.

Gupta, B. (2009) *Reason and Experience in Indian Philosophy*. Delhi: Indian Council of Philosophical Research.

Gupta, B. (2012) *An Introduction to Indian Philosophy: Perspectives on Reality, Knowledge and Freedom*. New York and Abingdon: Routledge.

Halbfass, W. (1988) '*Darśana, Ānvīkṣikī*, Philosophy' in *India and Europe: An Essay in Philosophical Understanding*. New York: SUNY, 263–86.

Hamilton, S. (2001) *Indian Philosophy: A Very Short Introduction*. Oxford: Oxford University Press.

Harimoto, K. (2014) *God, Reason, and Yoga: A Critical Edition and Translation of the Commentary Ascribed to Śaṅkara on Pātañjalayogaśāstra*. Hamburg: University of Hamburg.

Howard, V. (2019) 'Gender Conceptions in Indian Thought: Identity, Hybridity, Fluidity, Androgyny and Transcendence' in Howard, V. (ed.) *The Bloomsbury Research Handbook of Indian Philosophy and Gender*. London and New York: Bloomsbury Academic, 1–32.

Jacobsen, K. A. (ed.) (2012) *Yoga Powers: Extraordinary Capacities Attained through Meditation and Concentration*. Leiden: Brill.

Jakobsen, R. (1956) 'The Metaphoric and Metonymic Poles' in Jakobsen, R. and Halle, M. (eds.) *Fundamentals of Language*. Mouton: The Hague, 90–6.

Jain, A. (2015) *Selling Yoga: From Counterculture to Pop Culture*. Oxford: Oxford University Press.

Jain, A. (2020) *Peace, Love, Yoga: The Politics of Global Spirituality*. Oxford: Oxford University Press.

Jonker, A. (2021) 'Pāśupata Yoga and the Art of Dying: With Specific Reference to the *Pāśupatasūtra, Ratnaṭīkā* and *Skandapurāṇa*' in *Religions of South Asia* 15.1.

Keating, M. (2017) 'Metonymy and Metaphor as Verbal Postulation: The Epistemic Status of Non-Literal Speech in Indian Philosophy' in *Journal of World Philosophies* 2.1.

Kaviraj, G. (1923–24) "The Concept of *Pratibhā* in Indian Philosophy." *Annals of the Bhandarkar Oriental Research Institute* Vol 5.1, 1–18.

Khandelwal, M. (2010) *Women in Ochre Robes: Gendered Hindu Renunciation*. Albany: SUNY.

Kirloskar-Steinbach, M. and Kalmanson, L. (2021) *A Practical Guide to World Philosophies: Selves, Worlds, and Ways of Knowing*. London and New York: Bloomsbury Academic.

Kunjunni Raja, K. (1977) *Indian Theories of Meaning*. Madras: Adyar Library and Research Centre.

Larson, G. (1989) 'An Old Problem Revisited, the Relation between Sāṃkhya, Yoga, and Buddhism' in *Studien zur Indologie und Iranistik* 15.

Larson, G. (2018) *Classical Yoga Philosophy and the Legacy of Sāṃkhya with Sanskrit Text and English Translation of Pātañjala* Yogasūtra-s, Vyāsa Bhāṣya *and* Tattvavaiśāradī *of Vācaspatimiśra*. (MLBD Classical Systems of Indian Philosophy: 2) Delhi: Motilal Banarsidass.

Larson, G. and Bhattacharya, R. S. (eds.) (2008) *Yoga: India's Philosophy of Meditation*. Volume 12 *Encyclopedia of Indian Philosophies*. Delhi: Motilal Banarsidass Publishers Private Ltd.

Leggett, T. (trs.) (1990) *The Complete Commentary by Sankara on the Yoga Sutras: A Full Translation of the Newly Discovered Text*. London: Kegan Paul International.

Li, C. (2018) 'Sounding Out Différance: Derrida, Saussure and Bhartrhari' in *Philosophy East and West* 68.2: 447–59.

Lucyszyna, O. (2017) 'On the Notion of Linguistic Convention (*saṁketa*) in the *Yogasūtrabhāṣya*' in *Journal of Indian Philosophy*, 45.1, 1–19.

Lotman, Y. (1976) *Analysis of the Poetic Text*. Ann Arbor: University of Michigan Press.

Maas, P. (ed.) (2006) *Samādhipāda. Das erste Kapitel des Pātañjalayogaśāstra zum ersten Mal Kritisch Ediert*. Aachen: Studia Indologica Universitatis Halensis (GeisteskulturIndiens. Texte und Studien, 9).

Maas, P. (2013) 'A Concise Historiography of Classical Yoga' in Franco, E. (ed.) *Periodisation and Historiography of Indian Philosophy*. Vienna: University of Vienna, 53–90.

Maas, P. (2020a) 'Sarvāstivāda Buddhist Theories of Temporality and the Pātañjala Yoga Theory of Transformation' in *Journal of Indian Philosophy* 48.5.

Maas, P. (2020b) 'Pātañjalayogaśāstra' in Jacobsen, K., Malinar, A. and Narayanan, V. (eds.) *Brill's Encyclopedia of Hinduism Online*. URL: https://referenceworks.brillonline.com/browse/brill-s-encyclopedia-of-hinduism [accessed 02/11/2022].

Macdonald, A. (2009) 'Knowing Nothing: Candrakīrti and Yogic Perception' in Eli, Franco (ed.) *Yogic Perception, Meditation and Altered States of Consciousness*. Vienna: Verlag der Österreichischen Akademie der Wissenschaften, 133–68.

Maldonado-Torres, N., Vizcano, V., Wallace, J. and We, J. E. A. (2018) 'Decolonizing Philosophy' in Bhambra, G. K., Gebrial, D. and Niancolu, K. (eds.) *Decolonizing the University*. London: Pluto Press, 64–90.

Malinar, A. (2012) 'Yoga Practices in the *Bhagavadgītā*' in White, D. G. (ed.) *Yoga in Practice*. Princeton Readings in Religions. Princeton: Princeton University Press, 58–72.

Matilal, B. K. S. (1985) *Logic, Language and Reality*. Delhi: Motilal Banarsidass.

Matilal, B. K. S. (1990) *The Word and the World: India's Contributions to the Philosophy of Language*. Oxford: Oxford University Press.

Matilal, B. K. S. (1999) *The Character of Logic in India*. (ed. Ganeri and Tiwari). New York: SUNY.

Mbembe, A. (2016) 'Decolonizing the University: New Directions' in *Arts and Humanities in Higher Education* 15.1.

Mohanty, J. N. (2000) *Classical Indian Philosophy*. Lanham: Rowman and Littlefield.

Motegi, S. (2013) 'The Early History of Sāṃkhya Thought' in Franco, E. (ed.) *Historiography and Periodization of Indian Philosophy*. Vienna: De Nobili Research Library, 35–51.

Nicholson, A. (2010) *Unifying Hinduism: Philosophy and Identity in Indian Intellectual History*. New York: Columbia University Press.

O'Brien-Kop, K. (2018) 'Classical Discourses of Liberation: Shared Botanical Metaphors in Sarvāstivāda Buddhism and the Yoga of Patañjali' in *Religions of South Asia* 11.2–3: 123–57.

O'Brien-Kop, K. (2020) '*Dharmamegha* in Yoga and Yogācāra: The Revision of a Superlative Metaphor' in *Journal of Indian Philosophy* 48.4: 605–35.

O'Brien-Kop, K. (2021) *Rethinking 'Classical Yoga and Buddhism': Meditation, Metaphors and Materiality*. London: Bloomsbury Academic.

O'Brien-Kop, K. (2023) 'Defining Body and Mind: Yoga, Asceticism and Meditation' in Sathaye, Adheesh (ed.) *A Cultural History of Hinduism in the Classical Age 200 BCE–800CE*. London: Bloomsbury Academic.

Olivelle, P. (ed.) (2006) *Between the Empires: Society in India 300 BCE to 400 CE*. New York: Oxford University Press.

Olivelle, P. (2011) *Ascetics and Brahmins: Studies in Ideologies and Institutions*. London and New York: Anthem Press.

Osto, D. E. (2016) *Modern Sāṃkhya: Ancient Spirituality for the Contemporary Atheist*. New Zealand: Doug Osto.

Patton, L. (2008) '*Ṛṣis* Imagined across Difference: Some Possibilities for the Study of Conceptual Metaphor in Early India' in *The Journal of Hindu Studies* 1: 49–76.

Patton, L. (2013) 'Poetry, Ritual and Associational Thought in Early India and Elsewhere' in Pathak, S. (ed.) *Figuring Religions: Comparing Ideas, Images and Activities*. New York: SUNY, 179–98.

Perrett, R. (2007) 'Sāṃkhya-Yoga Ethics' in Bilimoria, P., Prabhu, J. and Sharma, S. (eds.) *Indian Ethics: Classical Traditions and Contemporary Challenges Volume 1*. London and New York: Routledge, 149–60.

Philips, S. (2019) 'Classical Indian Epistemology' *Stanford Encyclopedia of Philosophy* (on-line publication, entry revised March 2019). http://plato.stanford.edu/entries/epistemology-india/

Pollock, S. (2015) 'The Alternative Classicism of Classical India' Seminar 671 of India Seminar (July 2015). www.india-seminar.com. http://www.columbia.edu/cu/mesaas/faculty/directory/pollock_pub/The_alternative_classicism_of_classical%20India.pdf.

Pragya, P. (2020) 'Jain Yoga' in Newcombe, S. and O'Brien-Kop, K. (eds.) *The Routledge Handbook of Yoga and Meditation Studies*. London and New York: Routledge, 171–88.

Proferes, T. (2007) *Vedic Ideals of Sovereignty and the Poetics of Power*. New Haven: American Oriental Society.

Ranganathan, S. (ed.) (2017) *The Bloomsbury Research Handbook of Indian Ethics*. London and New York: Bloomsbury Academic.

Raghuramaraju, A. (2007) *Debates in Indian Philosophy: Classical, Colonial, and Contemporary*. Oxford: Oxford University Press.

Raghuramaraju, A. (2019) *Calibrating Western Philosophy for India: Rousseau, Derrida, Deleuze, Guattari, Bergson and Vaddera Chandidas*. London and New York: Routledge.

Raveh, D. (2012) 'Rethinking *Prajñā*: *Yogasūtra* 1.49 under a Philosophical Magnifying Glass' in *Exploring the Yogasūtra: Philosophy and Translation*. London and New York: Continuum, 61–74.

Rukmani, T. S. (trs.) (1981–1989) *Yogavārtikka of Vijñānabhikṣu: Text, with English Translation and Critical Notes along with the Text and English Translation of the Pātañjala Yogasūtra and Vyāsabhāṣya*, 4 vol. New Delhi: Munshiram Manoharlal.

Rukmani, T. S. (trs.) (2001) *Yogasūtrabhāṣyavivaraṇa of Śaṅkara: Vivaraṇa Text with English Translation, and Critical Notes along with Text and English Translation of Patañjali's Yogasūtras and Vyāsabhāṣya, Volumes 1 and 2*. New Delhi: Munshiram Manoharlal Publishers Pvt. Ltd.

Rukmani, T. S. (2011) 'Sāṃkhya-Yoga' in Edelglass, W. and Garfield, J. (eds.) *The Oxford Handbook of World Philosophy*. Oxford: Oxford University Press, 127–37.

Sathaye, A. (ed.) (2022) *A Cultural History of Hinduism in the Classical Age (200BCE–800CE)*. London and New York: Bloomsbury Publishing.

Sinha, B. (1983) *Time and Temporality in Sāṃkhya-Yoga and Abhidhaama Buddhism*. New Delhi: Munshiram Manoharlal Publishers.

Sinha, N. (trs.) (1923) *Vaiśeṣikasūtra of Kaṇāda Translated into English*. Allahabad: Vijaya Press.

Tubb, G. and Boose, E. (2007) *Scholastic Sanskrit: A Manual for Students*. American Institute of Buddhist Studies, New York: Columbia University.

Tzohar, R. (2018) *A Yogācāra Buddhist Theory of Metaphor*. Oxford: Oxford University Press.

van Norden, B. (2019) *Taking Back Philosophy: A Multicultural Manifesto*. New York: Columbia University Press.

Wezler, A. (1987) 'Zu der "Lehre von der 9 Ursachen" in Yogabhāṣya' in Falk, H. (ed.) *Hinduism und Buddhismus: Festschrift für Ulrich Schneider*. Freiburg: Heidwig Falk, 340–79.

Whicher, I. (2001) *The Integrity of the Yoga Darsana: A Reconsideration of Classical Yoga*. New York: SUNY.

Woods, J. (trs.) (1914) *The Yoga-System of Patañjali […] and the Comment Called Yoga-Bhāṣya Attributed to Veda-Vyāsa and the Explanation Called Tattva-Vaiśāradī of Vācaspati Miśra*. Cambridge, MA: Harvard Oriental Series.

Index